The Ultimate Guide To
The Art of
Drawing

igloobooks

igloobooks

Published in 2014
by Igloo Books Ltd
Cottage Farm
Sywell
NN6 0BJ
www.igloobooks.com

OCE001 0814
4 6 8 10 9 7 5 3
ISBN 978-1-78197-387-5

Written by Jennifer Sanderson

Printed and manufactured in China

Contents

Introduction

Art is all around us. It is in the beautiful painting that hangs on the wall and it is in the design of our new clothes and shoes. Art can be something aesthetically pleasing such as a striking sculpture or drawing, or it can be something as functional as the chair on which you are sitting.

Elements of art

All art, whether it is functional or designed to evoke an emotional reaction, contains certain elements. These elements of art are the building blocks that artists use, and without them, art would not be possible. They are:

• Line: a line is a continuous mark that is made on a surface by a moving point. Without line, we would not be able to draw shapes, objects or symbols – art would be impossible.

• Shape: this is an object that has only two dimensions: length and width. Geometric shapes such as circles, rectangles, squares, triangles and so on, have clear edges, while organic shapes have natural, less well-defined edges.

• Form: this is a three-dimensional object. Sculpture, by its nature, works with forms but those artists who draw or paint in two dimensions, seek to give their art the third dimension – depth.

• Space: this refers to distances or areas around, between or within the components of a piece. Space can be positive (white or light) or negative (black or dark), open or closed, shallow or deep and two-dimensional or three-dimensional. Sometimes space isn't actually within a piece, but the illusion of it is.

• Texture: this is used to describe the way a three-dimensional work feels when touched, or the visual 'feel' of a two-dimensional work.

• Value: this refers to the lightness or darkness of a colour. This is a crucial element when drawing in pencil because you need to use the grey of the pencil to create light and dark values.

• Colour: colour is used to give a drawing more vibrancy. It can also give a drawing the feeling of warmth and contrast.

Using these elements to draw

The aim of this book is to help you to feel confident to draw, whether it's to create something visually appealing that gives pleasure or something that can be used as a starting block to create something else. This book will teach you how to use the elements outlined opposite in your drawings, and how by using them, your drawing skills and confidence will improve.

INTRODUCTION

Can't Draw, Won't Draw

So often people say, 'I can't draw', and often, it's these same people that wish they could draw. While there are those who undoubtedly have an artistic talent, almost anyone who can hold a pencil can draw – most people just need a little help and some encouragement.

Step 1

Once you've taken the first step and decided that you want to try to draw, this book has all the information you will need. The first step is to read the section on what equipment you need to get started. You'll soon realise that you don't need a lot to draw – pencils and paper will be enough to begin with. Once you know that drawing is for you, and it's something you'd like to spend your free time doing, you can invest in better quality pencils and other drawing mediums and a sketchpad. For now, stick to the basic requirements and see how your drawing progresses over time.

Step 2

The next step is to read as much as possible about drawing techniques and styles so that you're familiar with the artistic terms used throughout this book. The reference section in the book also has short exercises to help you with art basics, such as drawing cylinders and positioning focal points.

Step 3

Once you have grasped the basic theory, you can put it all into practice by doing the step-by-step sketches. These step-by-step sketches will help you to draw different subjects, from dogs and violins to streets and helicopters. Each 'project' has four steps, the first shows you which basic shapes are used, in the second and third steps you are shown how to draw in the details, and in the fourth step, you shade your drawing and bring it to life. By following the steps, you'll be able to see that drawing is definitely not as daunting as it would seem, and more importantly, that it's a wonderful hobby that you can do anywhere, anytime.

Meet the Artists

The artwork in this book has been created by three different artists, Ray Burrow, Jo Blake and Ilias Arahovitis. Each one brings his or her own style to their art as you will see by the projects they worked on.

Jo Blake

Jo Blake has been an illustrator for more than 15 years. She specialises in a realistic style of illustration, and prefers to work traditionally in watercolour and black and white media.

Jo has worked mostly on teenage and children's books, both educational and storytelling.

As an artist, Jo is inspired to focus on apparently ordinary aspects of daily life, and from that create something special. Jo's principle skill and interest lies in figurative work and portraiture. You can see her work in the still life and portraiture step-by-step exercises.

Ray Burrows

Ray studied design at what is now the University of the Arts London, before working for a small illustration group. Since working as a freelance illustrator, Ray has drawn just about everything from microbes to the largest dinosaurs. Ray's art is featured in the machines, prehistoric and fantasy projects. The artist also drew the artwork for some of the theory section in the front of this book.

Ilias Arahovitis

Our third artist, Ilias Arahovitis was born in South Africa but now lives in Greece. His drawing style varies, depending on the project he is working on. Ilias can use both traditional and digital drawing techniques. In this book, Ilias' work can be seen in the architectural drawings, plant and garden exercises as well as the body section.

Getting Started

This chapter contains everything you need to know before you start to draw. You can find out what materials you will need and even how to use them. There is also a wealth of information on basic drawing skills, composition and perspective. This is the perfect introduction to get drawing!

Setting Up

While this book has all the information and exercises for you to start drawing, there are a few things you need to think about before you start to draw. These include buying your equipment, setting up a studio, and going outdoors.

Setting up a studio

There are tips later on in this book for setting up a studio or drawing space, but this is something you need to think about before you start, too. You will need somewhere quiet to draw, or at least somewhere free from distractions. Paying rent on a studio is an expensive commitment, so it's probably a good idea to find somewhere in your house that will be suitable. Set up boundaries if you share your house with other people, so they know that the area is your drawing space.

Buying equipment

By browsing art supply shops, you will see that not only is there a vast range of supplies available to buy, but there is a great disparity in price between them. Usually, materials and tools marked suitable for students are of a lesser quality. They may be fine to buy if you want to see if drawing is for you, but most times, you would be better off making an initial investment and buying better quality products. You can also buy materials online but in doing this, there are no sales assistants to help you to choose the most suitable products. It's a good idea to go into a shop initially and then, once you are familiar with the materials, source them online. When you are starting out, see if you can loan the bigger equipment, such as an easel or tilted worktop because they are costly investments to make if you're on a tight budget.

Going outdoors

While you can draw indoors, drawing outside can be a wonderful experience. Obviously you need to have suitable weather to do this – the last thing you want is your drawing being soaked by the rain or ripped by the wind! You'll need paper and pencils plus something on which to sit. While you can use any sized paper to draw on, for outdoor sketching, a smaller pad may be more convenient. A pad will also keep the pages together more easily than individual sheets. Store your pencils in some kind of pencil case, in which you can also pack your eraser and a craft knife to sharpen the lead. Take note of where you intend to draw as pencil sharpeners may be better than a sharp-bladed knife.

Artists' Materials

To draw, artists use a wide variety of materials. Some, such as pencils, pastels and charcoal are erasable and so somewhat more forgiving: mistakes can simply be 'wiped out'. Other materials, such as ink, chisel-tipped pens and brush pens are permanent and mistakes are harder to rectify.

Graphite pencils

Graphite pencils are available with hard, medium or soft leads. In most countries, the HB grading system is used to determine the hardness (H) or blackness (B) of the pencil. In this system, 10H is the hardest, while a 10B is the softest. In the United States, pencils are numbered: a #1 is equivalent to a B, #2 an HB, #3 an H and #4, a 2H.

Coloured pencils

Today, coloured pencils are becoming increasingly popular among artists. They are very versatile, especially those that are water soluble, which means they can be used with water. Artists use these pencils to draw their subject but then add water with a brush to soften the hard outlines and blend the colours.

Charcoal and Conté sticks

Although charcoal is one of the messier mediums with which to draw, many artists favour it. Different illustrative marks can be achieved, depending on how the stick is used. However, because charcoal smudges easily, a fixative must be used. The fixative 'fixes' the charcoal marks in position once the work is complete. Easier to use than charcoal, Conté sticks are a charcoal and wax compound. They also smudge easily so a fixing substance must be used to prevent smudging.

Pastels

Like pencils, pastels can be divided into hard and soft types. Hard pastels come in the form of compressed sticks, while soft pastels are usually chunky and crumbly. The particular appeal of soft pastels is their rich, dense colour, which is hard to achieve with other drawing materials.

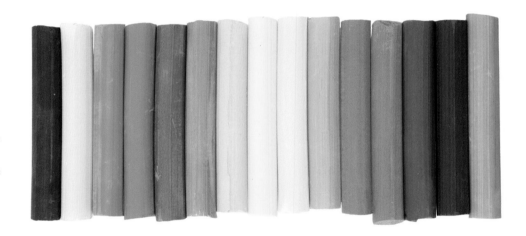

Pens

Pens are often categorised by the type of tip or nib that they have. While felt-tipped pens and fineliners are the most commonly used by artists, chisel-tipped pens now come in a wide range of colours and are becoming more and more popular with artists. With their flexible tip, brush pens can be used to create vibrant, colour-rich drawings.

Artists' Tools

In addition to artists' materials, such as pens, pencils and charcoal sticks, you will need some tools. These include the correct type of paper for the material you are using, erasers, sharpeners and fixing spray.

Paper

Artists' materials that are erasable, such as pencils and charcoal, are often referred to as 'dry', while those that are permanent, including pens and felt tips, are called 'wet'. To make the most of your drawing, you will need to choose the correct type of paper for your material. Dry materials do not work particularly well on smooth paper because they need something on which to grip. Grainier paper adds texture and character to your finished artwork. For pencil drawings, look for paper marked as such. Often this will come in a sketchpad. If your chosen material falls in the 'wet' group, you will need a smooth paper. By using a smoother paper you'll ensure that the grain of the paper doesn't interfere with or catch onto your pen as you draw.

Pencil sharpeners

You will need to keep your pencils sharp. To do this, you can use an ordinary pencil sharpener but make sure you are able to sharpen a long shaft of graphite. This may be more easily achieved by using a craft knife. Craft knives allow you to shave the tip of the pencil to create not only a sharp point, but also to bare more graphite, making the pencil ideal for shading.

Erasers

For dry materials, you will also need erasers. These are used not only to remove and correct unwanted lines, but they are also used to create highlights. The most versatile eraser is a kneadable eraser. This can be kneaded so that it's quite malleable and can then be moulded into a point to make adjustments. A plastic or vinyl eraser will rub out even the darkest graphite. Keep a craft knife and sandpaper handy to shape your eraser.

Fixing sprays

If you intend to keep your artwork for any length of time, you will need to 'fix' it in place, using a fixative. While some people suggest using hair lacquer, if you want your artwork to last, don't economise on your fixing spray. Look for spray that is specifically suited to the material that you're using. For pencil artwork, you can use any marked 'archival', 'matte finish' or even those marked for pastels and charcoal.

Finding a Workstation

One of the great things about drawing is that you can do it wherever and whenever you like. However, drawing and completing a piece takes considerable time, so you need to ensure you are comfortable as you work. Setting up a work area is very important.

Choosing a work area

Wherever you decide your workstation will be, pay careful attention to your surroundings. Your work area should be a place that inspires creativity – avoid noisy areas, such as the middle of your kitchen or general living areas. Choose somewhere peaceful and calm and that does not have distractions such as a ringing telephone or loud television.

Tables and chairs

Your chair needs to be comfortable. Try to find a height-adjustable chair so that you are able to sit properly and correctly while you draw. A chair with wheels is useful because you can move backwards and forwards easily if you need to. A drafting table is an adjustable worktop with a slanted top. They are great if you aim to draw extensively and are serious about your craft, but can be an expensive investment if you're just starting out. You could improvise and create your own sloping surface by propping up a piece of wood with some books. Creating a slanted worktop is important – if you work on a flat surface, the top will be further away from you than the bottom, and your drawing could be out of proportion.

Light

Good light is essential for good art. You need to be able to see your art clearly and without your eyes becoming sore or tired. If it's possible, try to set up your workstation near a window that offers natural light during the day. You'll need to be near an artificial light source on dull or overcast days and at night, but stay away from fluorescent lights because they can cause headaches. You will probably also need a study lamp with a flexible neck to focus light on your drawings.

Storing and displaying

You will also need somewhere to store your materials.
A cart on wheels will keep all your paper, pencils and
other drawing equipment neat and tidy until you need
it. You'll need drawers or folders in which to keep your
art: stashing them under a rug or bed is not a good
idea! To display your art, you can peg them onto a
board or an easel. It can be inspirational to easily
see your finished art and show off your pieces.

Techniques for Drawing Well

Drawing can be time consuming and, like any activity in which you sit in the same position for a long time, it can lead to aching muscles and headaches. To help alleviate these symptoms, you need to sit properly and hold your pencil or other drawing material comfortably and correctly.

Perfect posture

Comfort is crucial – if you're uncomfortable or in a painful sitting position, your art will suffer for it. Keep your body straight but slightly inclined forward. If you can, adjust the height of your chair so that your feet are flat on the floor, or on a footstool, with your knees bent at right angles.

If you're sitting properly and your table is set up correctly, you should be able to see your drawing without bending your lower back. Try to keep your eyes at a good distance from your work. If you're too close to your work, you won't be able to see it properly. Once you're sitting properly, make sure that you take regular breaks to stretch your muscles.

Scribe's grip

How do you hold your pencil? Most beginners will hold their pencil in a scribe's grip. This is the grip you were probably taught to use when writing. The fundamental problem with this grip is that writing and drawing are two very different activities. Writing uses the fingers and wrist while the whole arm, including the shoulder, are used for drawing.

Pen grip

Instead of using the scribe's grip, try to draw using the pen grip. To do this, hold your pencil as you would a pen to write, but move your fingers much further from the tip of the pencil. This grip will give you more control when drawing smaller features, but it is not ideal for working with the side of your pencil or for creating broad strokes. For this, you need to use a violin bow grip.

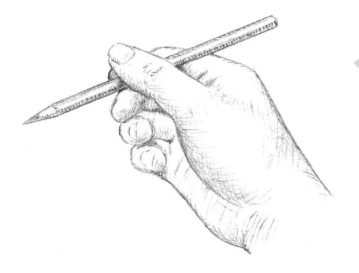

Violin bow grip

To achieve a violin bow grip, hold your pencil with the thumb against all four fingers. This grip will take the control away from your fingers and move it to your wrist and arm at the shoulder.

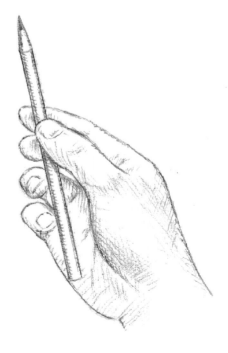

Sketching Basic Shapes

All objects, from vases and flowers to horses and dogs, can be broken down into a few basic shapes. If you are able to see these basic shapes in everything you draw, you'll be amazed at how easily the rest of the drawing follows.

What shapes?

The basic shapes to look for are squares, rectangles, triangles, cones, cylinders, circles and ovals. Remember, the shapes that you create don't have to be perfectly drawn. Sometimes, an oval may be a little squashed and triangles can look very different, depending on the size of the angles and the lengths of the sides.

Head

To draw the perfect horse, start by drawing your grid. Look at the shape of the horse's head. What shapes can you see? Draw these shapes.

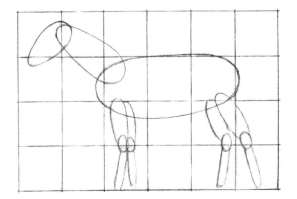

Body

Now you can draw the basic shapes of the horse's body and legs. Notice how the horse's legs aren't just one shape, there is a joint in the the middle, and the top of the leg is wider than at the bottom.

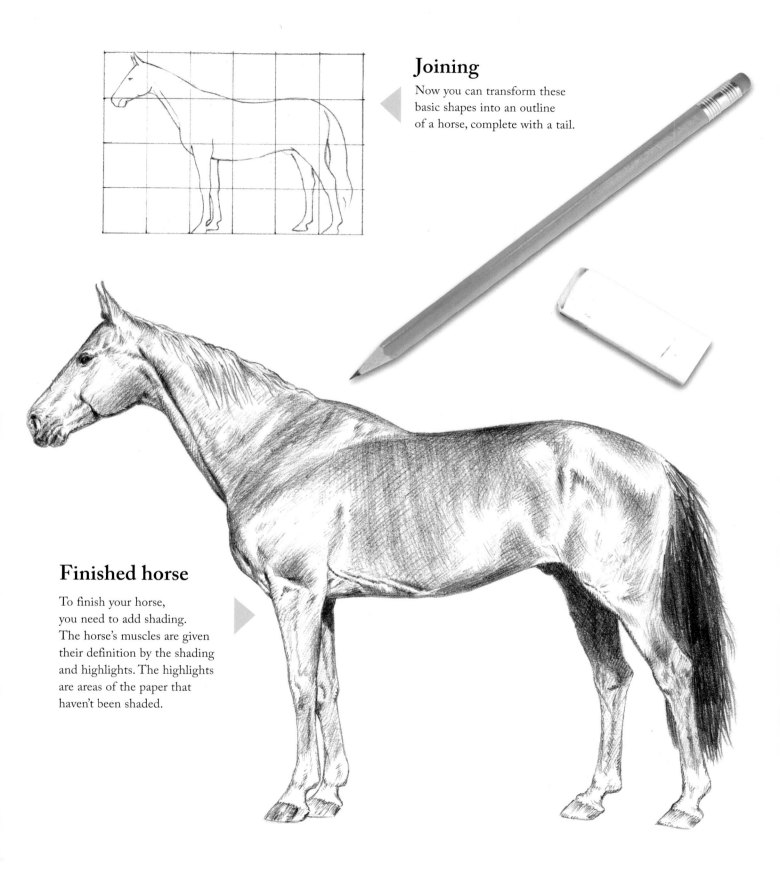

Joining

Now you can transform these basic shapes into an outline of a horse, complete with a tail.

Finished horse

To finish your horse, you need to add shading. The horse's muscles are given their definition by the shading and highlights. The highlights are areas of the paper that haven't been shaded.

Drawing Ellipses

Look at a plate from overhead. Can you see that it is a circle? Now look at the same plate from
a sitting position. The shape you see now is an ellipse. Ellipses are circles drawn at an angle or in
perspective. They are the curves you see at the rim of rounded objects such as cups, glasses and vases.

How to draw an ellipse

When you draw an ellipse, the two sides should be symmetrical, both vertically
and horizontally. The ellipse should be vertical at the left and right points and
horizontal at the top and bottom points. To check the symmetry of your
ellipse, hold your drawing against a mirror or turn it upside down.

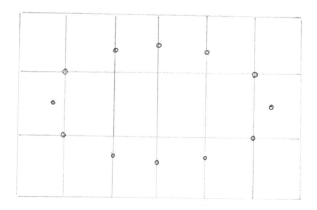

Step 1

There are several ways that you can draw an ellipse, this is our artist's preferred method. To start with, draw a grid. Now mark two dots in the middle of your grid at the same distance from the top and bottom lines. Then mark off two dots at the same distance from either side. Add two more dots between each of these four dots.

Step 2

Check the symmetry of your ellipse by drawing a vertical line at each end. Use a ruler to do this.

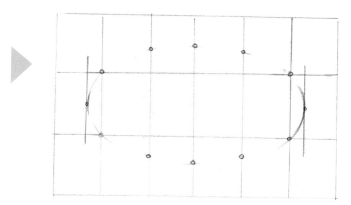

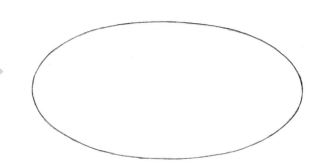

Step 3

Now you can join the dots! Use a steady hand to do this so that you create a smooth shape.

Step 4

To finish your ellipse, rub out the lines of the grid and the dots that you drew in the first step.

Tone

Sometimes referred to as value or shading, tone is the measure of light and dark in a drawing.
Tones range from white through to grey and on to a very dark black. They give your artwork the
illusion of depth, thus making it appear three-dimensional and 'lifting' it off the page.

Finding the light

In order to accurately capture the tones of a drawing, you will need to understand light because light will show
you where to shade and how much shading is needed. Light can come from a natural light source, such as the Sun
shining through a window, or an artificial light source, such as a lamp that has been set up near a still life table.

Shadows

Highlights

The part of an object closest to the light source is usually the brightest and lightest. These bright
areas are called the highlights. Highlights can be created by leaving the white of the paper to show
through or by using a kneadable eraser to remove shading. Closest to the highlights, are the lighter
tones. The objects further from the light source are the medium and then the darkest tones. These
will need darker shading. A cast shadow is a dark section on an adjacent surface that receives
little or no light. These shadows are darkest next to the object and lighter as you move away.

Picking your pencils

Different pencils create lighter and darker shading. A 2H pencil will give a lighter tone while a 6B pencil will create a very dark shade. You could also use the same pencil and apply different amounts of pressure when holding it. If using this method, always begin with light, loose strokes, and increase the pressure to produce darker tones.

Layering up

The density of shading used will also affect the tone – the denser the shading, the darker the tone. However, repeatedly shading in the same direction can give art a 'blocky' look. To smooth out the tone, rub gently over your drawing in a light circular motion with your fingertip. This will give your art a smoother finish.

Hatching and Cross-Hatching

Shading can be created in several ways. These include hatching and cross-hatching. You can use one method in a drawing or a combination of both, depending on your subject and your personal preference.

Hatching

Hatching is probably the most widely used method of shading. This involves drawing straight or curved lines next to, or parallel to, each other. These lines are called a set, and they can be close together or further apart, depending on the effect you wish to achieve. For lighter tones, the lines need to be far apart but for darker tones, they should be closer together.

Cross-hatching

Cross-hatching allows for a smoother transition of values. Here, one set of lines is drawn at a right angle to another set so that the lines overlap. The smaller the gap between the lines, the denser the shading or darker the tone. Cross-hatching is especially useful for ink drawings because artists cannot make the ink lighter or darker.

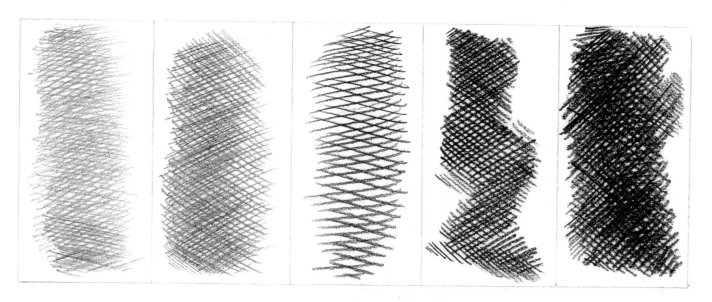

Creating Texture

Smooth, rough, spiky, furry and bumpy are just some of the textures that artists recreate to achieve a tactile quality in their drawings. This gives the work the illusion of a surface. By adjusting the tones of a drawing, artists can create different textures. Hatching and cross-hatching, loops and squiggles and pointillism are just some of the techniques you can use.

Hatching and cross-hatching

As well as using hatching and cross-hatching to add tone to a drawing, you can use them to add texture. These two techniques are usually used to create a smoother, more muted texture.

Loops and squiggles

To create a softer texture, artists use a combination of loops and squiggles. When these are closer together, the texture looks smoother than when the loops and squiggles are further apart.

Pointillism

Using dots to create a pattern or texture is called pointillism. This technique works well on lighter shaded areas. The more dots you use, the more textured the surface.

Paper

While you will need to use a rougher paper for your graphite to stick to the surface, different papers will create different textures. If you use paper with a rougher surface, your final drawing will be rougher.

Dents and holes

You can also use different objects to create dents and holes to give different surfaces. Any tool that makes a mark, from an eraser to a thick, blunt needle, can be used to add texture to your drawing.

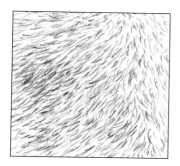

Fur

To create a furry texture, use a combination of short and long lines in the same direction as the fur grows.

Hair

Because hair is similar to fur, you can use a similar technique to the one used to draw fur.

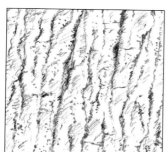

Bark of tree

Broken, uneven lines with varying spaces between give the illusion of a rough bark.

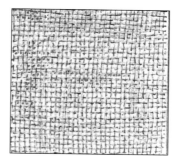

Fabric

Use cross-hatching with the lines slightly apart to create the illusion of fabric.

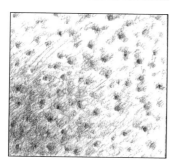

Orange peel

As well as smoothness, orange peel has dimples that need to be captured.

Brick

The surface of a brick has cracks and lines in it that you can capture using shading.

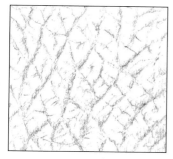

Skin

If you look closely at your skin, you will see that it isn't smooth, but rather has a mesh-like appearance.

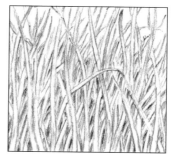

Grass

The bottom of the grass is denser so it is shown by using darker tones than the top of the blades.

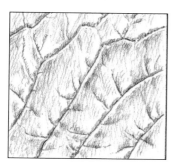

Leaves

The veins of a leaf need to be drawn darker than the background.

Snake skin

By shading the edges of each diamond shape darker, the scales are given depth.

Using a Grid

A grid is like an artist's safety net because, instead of focusing on an entire picture, a grid allows you to work on a drawing square by square. Grids are especially useful when creating still life pieces or when drawing from photographs.

What is a grid?

A grid is piece of a cardboard or acetate with horizontal and vertical lines drawn on it to create squares. Grids can be made up of any number of squares, but all the squares must be equal in size. When using a cardboard grid, an artist places it behind the object or collection of objects he or she is drawing. An acetate or plastic grid can be placed over the photograph that is being copied. The artist then plots the same number of equal-sized squares on his or her paper. Any part of the object's outline that falls into a certain square on the big grid is drawn on the corresponding square on the artist's sheet of paper.

How to use a grid

Step 1: measure the height and width of the object in the photograph. Use these measurements to draw a grid of even squares onto a sheet of acetate.

Step 2: place the grid behind or over your photograph so that the entire object is in the grid. Secure the grid.

Step 3: draw a corresponding grid on your sheet of paper. It must have exactly the same number of rows and columns as the acetate grid.

Step 4: draw the subject square by square so that it matches the photograph.

Step 5: erase the grid.

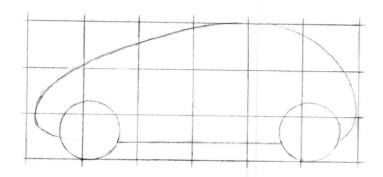

Step 1

Once you have drawn the grid over your photograph, draw a grid with the same number of squares on your paper. Now draw the basic shapes that you can see.

Step 2

Now add more detail to your car's basic shape so that it starts to look like a car.

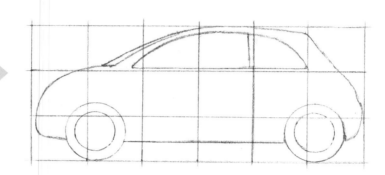

Step 3

Now you can add the values to give the car its three-dimensional shape. The tyres are the darkest because they are made from rubber and the inside of the car is in shadow so that, too, will need to be darker. The bodywork is metallic so there are lots of highlights. By shading underneath the car, the car is grounded.

Composition

Artists position things in their drawings to achieve balance – all the component or individual parts need to work together. This 'balance' is called composition. A well-balanced drawing will captivate the viewer.

Paper shape

One of the most basic aspects of composition is choosing the size and shape of your piece of paper. To use the correct sized paper, everything must fit on the paper but the paper cannot be too large – if it is, the viewer's eyes will not be able to focus on the drawing. The shape of the paper can be landscape or portrait, horizontal or vertical. Again, everything needs to fit on the paper within the chosen size.

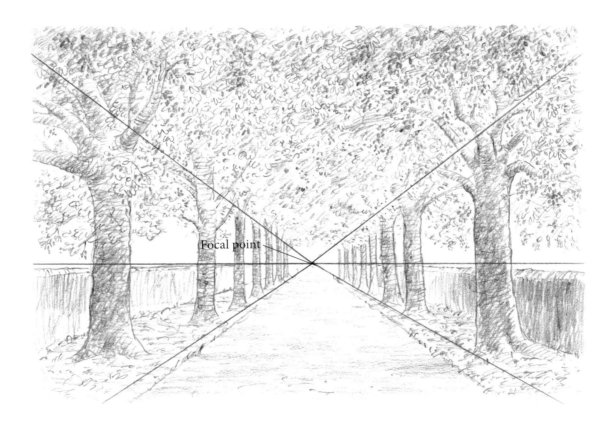

Focal point

Focusing on focal points

Once you have chosen the size and shape of your paper, you need to decide where to draw the focal point. The focal point in a drawing is the point to which the viewer's eyes are drawn. The focal point is usually the main subject of a drawing. Sometimes, there are two focal points. The secondary focal point must work with the main focal point to achieve a balance.

Drawing your focal point

If you position your focal point exactly in the centre of your piece of paper, or if you divide your paper in half with a tall object in the middle, your drawing will have very little impact. Similarly, if the same sized objects are placed equidistant on either side of the centre line, your drawing will be rather boring.

To achieve a good balance, one of the most commonly used theories for positioning a focal point is called the 'golden ratio' or 'golden mean'. The golden ratio was discovered by the Greek mathematician, Euclid. He worked out that a sequence of numbers (3, 5, 8, 13, 21…) gave a series of ratios. This means that if a line is drawn by combining two successive numbers in the ratio, for example 5 and 8 to give a line of 13, and divided into the two component lengths (one of 5 and one of 8), the ratio of the smaller part (5) to the larger part (8) is the same as the ratio of the larger part (8) to the whole (13). So:

'C' (A+B) is to 'A' as 'A' is to 'B'

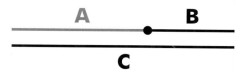

If you divide your paper up according to the golden ratio, where the vertical and horizontal lines of the ratio intersect (usually a third of the way in and a third of the way up or down), you will find one of the better places to position your focal point. Once you know where to draw it, you need to make the focal point stand out. This can be done by using more detailed shading or by adding darker values. The focal point should also be the largest item in the drawing.

Proportion

Proportion is the relationship between the size, location, or amount of one element of the whole to another element of the whole. Good proportion adds balance and harmony to a drawing. However, it is often easier to pinpoint something that is out of proportion than something that is in proportion.

Standard proportion

The correct height, width and depth of an object compared to its surroundings is called standard proportion. One of the best examples of standard proportion is found on the human body, in particular the human face. All faces are roughly oval. The width of the oval is approximately five eyes wide. The eyes are positioned about halfway down the oval. The bottom of the nose is as wide as the gap between the inner corners of the eyes. The pupils of the eyes usually line up with the corners of the mouth. A person's ears are found between the eye line and the imaginary line drawn at the bottom of the nose, the 'nose line'. By following these guidelines when you draw a face, the face will be in proportion and look balanced.

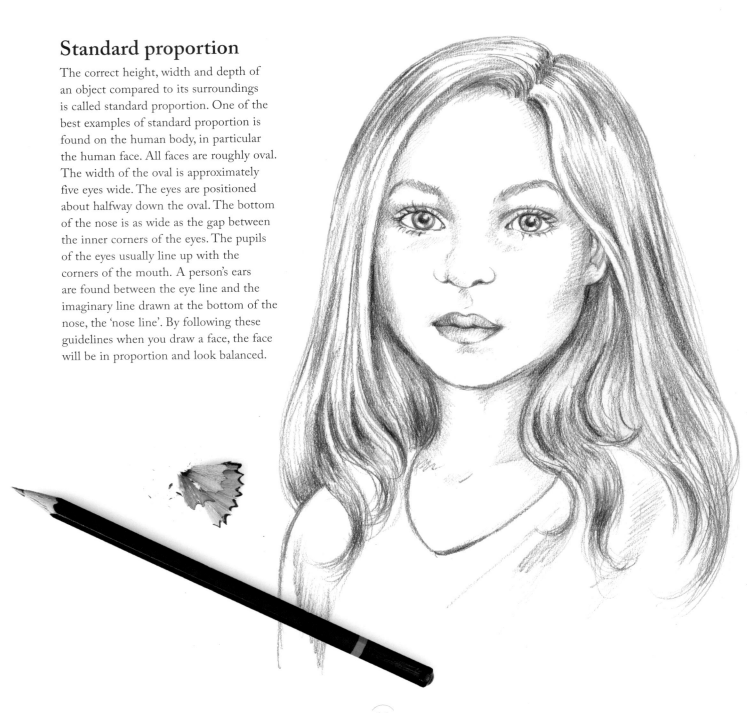

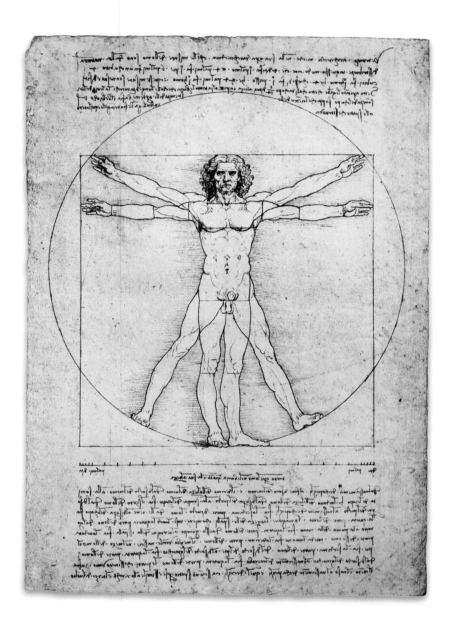

Drawing in proportion

To make sure that you draw your subject, regardless of what it is, in proportion, there are simple steps you can follow. Start by looking for something in your subject that you can measure. For example, an apple in a still life or the length of your subject's head. Once you've worked out the size of this object, measure the rest of your subject in relation to it. This will mean working with ratios, so to make things simple, use ratios that are easy to work with, such as 1:2 and 1:4. Remember when you are measuring, to hold your arm straight and stand at the same point each time. For good measure, check everything twice before you mark your paper and then check again after you've marked your paper – if something's not right, remeasure until it is!

Cropping

Cropping is a technique that involves a truncation, or cutting off, of some
parts of the subject. It brings the viewer closer to the subject of a drawing and
creates drama. However, cropping can make it difficult to balance a drawing.

Cropping and composition

As discussed earlier, when you're beginning a new drawing, you need to look at the size and shape of the subject
and choose your paper size accordingly. You know now that to achieve a good composition and balance in your art,
the focal point should ideally be on the 'golden mean' and by dividing your paper accordingly, you can work out
where this is. However, if there is a lot of white space or unwanted objects around your focal point, you may
want to crop these so that you guide your viewer's eye to the focal point. By cropping out the white space
or unwanted objects, you will bring the viewer closer to the subject, but will your drawing still look balanced?

Judging composition

One of the best ways to judge whether a drawing is balanced or not is to complete a thumbnail sketch in which you draw your subject as you'd like to crop it. Then, stand back a little and look at your drawing. If you feel your paper looks too crowded, it is likely that you've cropped too closely. If you've cropped too closely, your subject may also be losing its shape or some of the values or tones that define it. If your subject grabs your attention and lures you into the drawing, you've cropped successfully.

To the edge

Another way to crop your drawing and focus on the subject, is to let part of your drawing run to one or more of the paper's edges. This will change the composition of your drawing. Depending on the subject, it may also result in a triangular composition that does not work for your subject. Again, stand back and evaluate the balance and composition.

Using a Viewfinder

A viewfinder is an adjustable frame that enables you to see the subject of your drawing from various viewpoints. You can use a viewfinder to plan any composition, whether you are drawing from a photograph, a section of your garden or a still life that you've set up.

Make a viewfinder

Viewfinders are readily available at good art shops, but if you don't want to buy a viewfinder, you can easily make your own. To do this, you will need a large sheet of neutral-coloured cardboard. Neutral card is the best choice because a brightly coloured card may detract from the subject of your drawing. Using a ruler, measure two 'L' shapes exactly the same size. Cut out the shapes using a sharp craft knife and ruler. It will be useful to make a selection of different-sized viewfinders – you can use smaller ones for working from photographs and larger ones for working outdoors.

Using your viewfinder

Once you've decided on the subject of your artwork, place one 'L' over the other to create either a square or rectangular viewfinder. Now slide both 'L's to adjust the size and shape of your view through the viewfinder. When you find a suitable composition, use tape or paper clips to hold the frame together. Larger viewfinders will need to be anchored so that you have two free hands with which to draw. You can do this by cutting out a section from a Styrofoam cup and slotting the viewfinder into it. The image you see through the viewfinder is the image you will draw. If you are drawing from a photograph, you can mark the inside four corners of the viewfinder on your photograph so that you know what you need to draw.

View through a window

When drawing landscapes, instead of using cardboard frames to make a viewfinder, you can use windows and doors to create an interesting view. This means that instead of trying to draw an entire garden, you can look through the window and draw just the area that you see.

Drawing with a viewfinder

When drawing while using a viewfinder, it is very important to keep your head, the viewfinder, and the subject of your drawing all exactly the same distances and in the same places while you draw. If things move, the proportions of your drawing will change, quite possibly without you realising it.

Measuring Angles

As students, most people would have used a protractor to measure angles as part of a lesson in mathematics. At the time, this skill may have seemed very irrelevant, but measuring angles is a vital skill to render accurate drawings.

Drawing precisely

When you measure angles, you need to do this methodically so that your measurements are as accurate as possible. Each time you measure a part of your subject, stand or sit in exactly the same place and at the same height. In the same way you worked with proportion, measure at least twice before you mark your paper.

Protractors

To use a protractor accurately, find a reference line against which you can measure your angles. Hold your protractor in front of your image and check the angle of the part of your subject you are measuring. While protractors will give you very precise measurements, other tools and methods you can use may not be as precise, but may be easier to use.

Pencil power

There are two ways you can use pencils to measure angles. The first method of measurement uses just one pencil, while for the second method, you'll need two pencils. If you're using one pencil, find a vertical line in your subject or behind your subject, such as a door frame. This is your reference line. Now, tilt your pencil to align with the feature you are measuring. Using the horizontal line of your paper, keep your hand steady as you transfer the measurement to your paper. If you want to use two pencils to measure angles, hold them both in the same hand. One pencil should be vertical while you align the second with the part of the subject you are measuring. If you find this second method helpful, you can fashion your own cardboard measuring tool by taking two strips of cardboard and joining them together with a split pin.

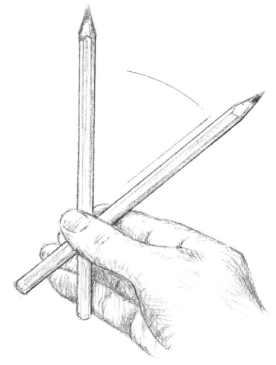

Using circles

Another way to measure angles is to think of your subject as having 12 equal segments, much the same as the face on an analogue clock. Measure the angles against the 12 segments. If you're using a viewfinder already, you can add crosshairs to it and use them to measure the angles.

Perspective

One of the challenges of drawing is to create the illusion of three dimensions. Without perspective, this is impossible to do. Perspective is a method of representing subjects and parts of the subject so that they recede in the distance and appear to be further away than they actually are.

Linear perspective

Although sometimes called geometric perspective, linear perspective is usually what people mean when they talk about perspective drawing. Before you can understand perspective, you need to know some basic terminology:

• Horizon line: this is an imaginary horizontal line drawn at eye level. The horizon line divides your line of vision when you look straight ahead of you.

• Vanishing point: this is the point on the horizon line where the straight lines of an object converge and seem to disappear or vanish.

Placing your subject

Where you place your subject in relation to the horizon line in your drawing will have a great effect on the composition of your artwork. For example, if your drawing is at eye level, the viewer will feel as though the drawing is an extension of his or her space, and he or she will view the image in relation to their body. Because the viewer's eye is naturally drawn towards the horizon line, a high eye level will focus more attention on the middle and rear areas of your drawing. A low eye level means that more attention will be focused on the rear area of the drawing, allowing more space to draw the sky. Having a large area of sky can help to create a specific mood in a drawing.

More About Perspective

Linear perspective can be achieved by using either one-point, two-point
or three-point perspective. Drawing cubes and boxes will help you to
understand how one-point and two-point perspective work in practise.

One-point perspective

In one-point perspective, the frontal
face of an object is closest to the viewer
and the edges converge and disappear
at a single vanishing point.

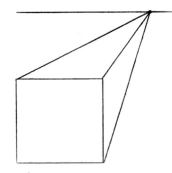

Step 1

Draw horizon line and
mark vanishing point
on line. Draw an
outline of a square.

Step 2

Draw lines to link
the vanishing point
and the three corners
of the square.

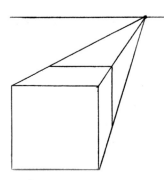

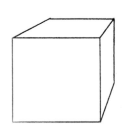

Step 3

Draw horizontal and
vertical lines to complete
the back of the cube.

Step 4

Use an eraser to rub
out the lines so that
you are left with a cube.

Two-point perspective

In two-point perspective, it will seem as though you are looking at an object or scene from one corner, with two sets of parallel lines moving away from you. Because each set of parallel lines has its own vanishing point, in two-point perspective, there are two vanishing points.

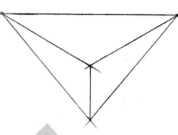 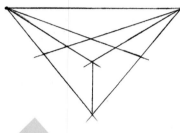 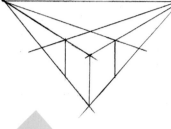

Step 1

Draw a horizon line with vanishing points at both ends of the horizon line. Draw a vertical line in the middle of the horizon line but lower down. Join the vertical line at the top and bottom with the vanishing points.

Step 2

Draw two more diagonal lines that go back to the vanishing points, so that your drawing looks like the one above.

Step 3

Using the lines you drew in step two, draw two vertical lines where the lines intersect. These will be the sides of your box.

Step 4

Use an eraser to rub out the lines so that you are left with your box.

Three-point perspective

Three-point perspective is most often used in drawing buildings and other structures that are viewed from a low or high eye level. If the subject of a drawing is above the horizon line, the view will be looking up at the subject. This will make a building seem very tall. Similarly, the viewer will be looking down at the subject if the subject is drawn below the horizon line. Three-point perspective uses three sets of parallel lines and three vanishing points.

Horizon Line

Vanishing Point

Drawing Cylinders

Once you have mastered drawing an ellipse and you understand perspective, you can use this skill and knowledge to draw a cylinder. A cylinder is two ellipses with a rectangle. Cylinders feature in still lifes; vases, cups, mugs and bottles are all cylindrical in shape.

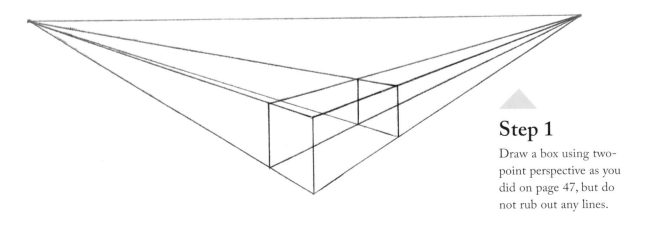

Step 1

Draw a box using two-point perspective as you did on page 47, but do not rub out any lines.

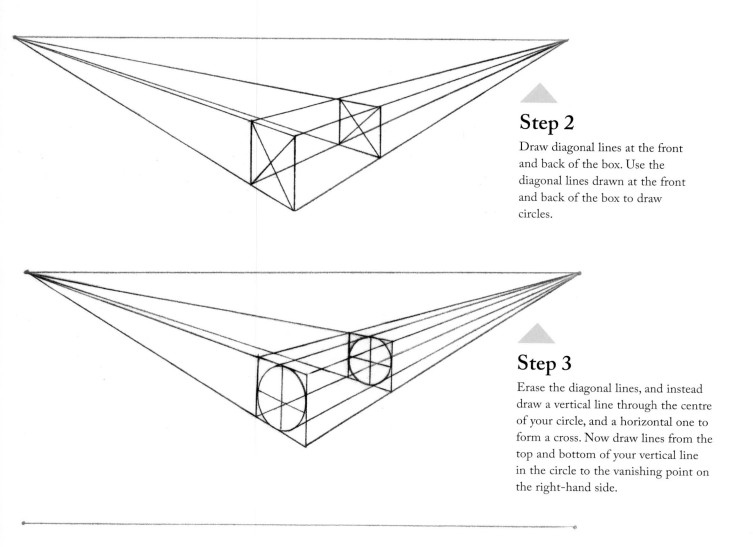

Step 2

Draw diagonal lines at the front and back of the box. Use the diagonal lines drawn at the front and back of the box to draw circles.

Step 3

Erase the diagonal lines, and instead draw a vertical line through the centre of your circle, and a horizontal one to form a cross. Now draw lines from the top and bottom of your vertical line in the circle to the vanishing point on the right-hand side.

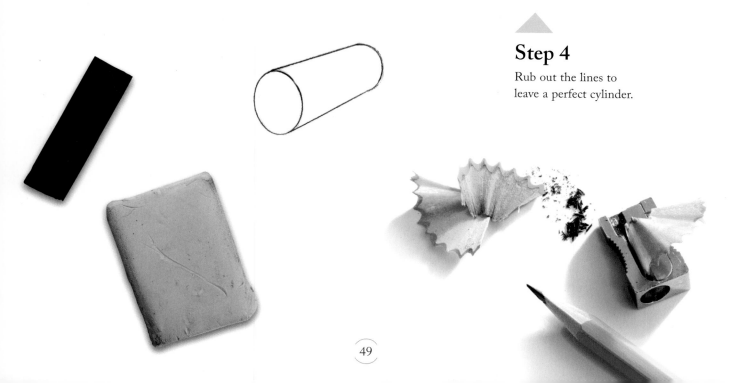

Step 4

Rub out the lines to leave a perfect cylinder.

A Matter of Subject

Now that you know and understand the theory, it's time to apply it and start drawing. This chapter will help you to choose a subject. There are also step-by-step examples to help you to develop your drawing skills.

Choosing a subject

By now you've worked through this book and so you know what perspective is, you can place your subject so that the composition 'works' and you know a 2B from a 4H, but how do you use all this new-found knowledge to draw something? The first thing you need to do is to find a willing subject to draw. Often, this is one of the hardest things about starting out.

Draw your current life

It has always been said that writers should write about what they know. In many ways, the same can be said of artists. This is because if you draw what you know about, your familiarity will fuel your confidence. If you are confident before you start to draw, you will feel bolder with your pencils or charcoal and more inclined to try something new. Knowing your subject will give you an innate knowledge of the finer details, details that are invaluable to drawing precisely and accurately. However, always drawing what you know about, may lead to boredom, and sometimes you will need a change in subject.

Draw what interests you

For many people, there is something that fascinates them and that they find interesting. If you're interested in something, draw it! Even if it is something that you don't know very well, as long as you find it interesting you will enjoy drawing it. You will, however, need to study it carefully before you start to draw it.

Draw what is around you

Many people are surrounded by subjects worthy of drawing without even realising it. Subjects like your pets, a bowl of fruit that sits on your kitchen counter or a musical instrument make for interesting things to draw. Try to find subjects that are rich or varied in colour, subjects that capture the light in an interesting way or subjects that have unusual angles. If you have a garden, there are undoubtedly many things you could draw, from flowers in bloom to birds and insects that live there.

Know your limits

While there may be many things that inspire you and that you want to draw, it is always worthwhile knowing or acknowledging your abilities. If you tackle something that is incredibly complex and you are just starting out, chances are you'll be put off and frustrated before the drawing is complete. Accept your level and although you should try to improve it with each drawing you do, remember that it's not a race to get there. Practise the basic skills and the more difficult skills will follow.

Pomegranate

The inside of a pomegranate is a deep red colour and filled with small seeds suspended in a bright, jelly-like substance. To capture these seeds and give them depth and shape, you need to use shading.

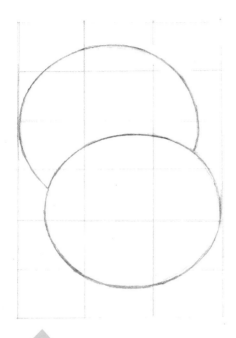

Step 1

Cut one of your pomegranates in half so that the little seeds are exposed. Position the fruit as you'd like them to be – because of their shape and the contrast between the cut and whole fruit, our artist has positioned them one in front of the other.
Now draw your grid. Once you have worked out where on the grid your pomegranates will sit, draw the simple circular shapes that make up the outline of the pomegranates.

Step 2

Add details such as the top, or stamen of the fruit and the segments. While the outer skin of the pomegranates looks smooth from a distance, up close, the skin has marks and is textured. To achieve this texturing, our artist has started with a layer of hatching, with the lines quite far apart.

Step 3

The little seeds and jelly-like nectar will need to be added to the outline of the cut fruit. Notice how the seeds are all round and fit perfectly into the segments. Add more tone to the outer edges by making the lines darker. You can do this with a softer pencil or by adding more pressure with the same pencil. Add further hatching to the fruits so that they start to get more depth.

Step 4

Look carefully at your fruit to see where the light is falling. The brighter, lighter areas are the highlights, so start with these. To capture these, the white of your paper will need to show through. To give the seeds their definition, our artist has shaded between them. Those farthest from the light source are darkest and will need more shading. Layers of hatching and cross hatching have been added to the uncut fruit to give the skin its texture. Where the light has created shadow, you'll need to use a long shaft of graphite to create this effect.

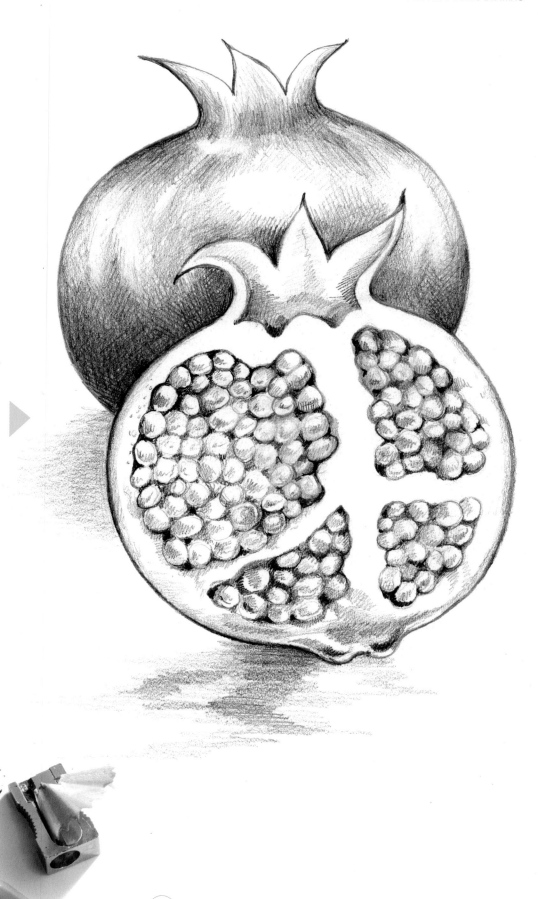

Roses

The rose is one of the most popular flowers. There are several elements to a rose, including the petals, thorns and leaves. Each element has its own characteristics and therefore its own texture. This rose has created strong shadows that the artist has captured to give the rose a realistic appearance.

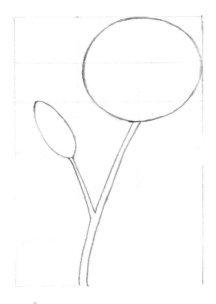

Step 1

Try to find a rose that has a full, open flower and a bud because it makes for a more interesting drawing. Draw your grid. Look carefully at the flower to see the shapes of the thorns, leaves and stem. You'll see the open flower can be broken down into a circle and the bud is oval in shape. Decide where you want to crop the stem of the flower so that you know how much of it to include in your drawing. Start by drawing the petals of the open flower.

Step 2

Now fill in the details of the flower and the bud, as well as the basic outline of the leaves. Use the full size of your grid but try to keep the leaves in proportion to the rest of the flower. The leaves often weigh down the stems, causing them to bend a little.

Step 3

Darken your outline of the petals and bud as well as the stem by using a soft pencil. Rose leaves are jagged around the edge, so add these details as well as the veins of the leaves. You can add the thorns too at this stage.

Step 4

Once you've added the details, you can start to shade your drawing. To capture the folds of the petals, you will need to use darker shading around the fold lines. The flower and bud are also darker at the base compared to the tip of the petals. To capture the shape of the thorns, the bottom curve is shaded darker than the top curve. Notice where your light source is creating shadows as you will need to add these, too.

Vase

The lip of a vase is also an ellipse, so you may need to practise drawing this shape before you draw your vase. Once you have mastered this basic shape, you can use your vase as a container for a bunch of flowers, creating a more complex still-life drawing.

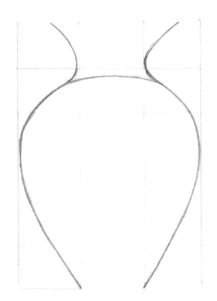

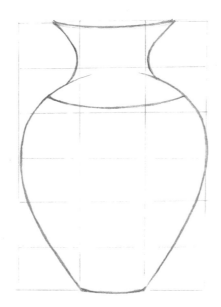

Step 1

Once you have drawn your grid, you can start by drawing the two shapes that make up your vase. The body of this vase is oval but your vase could be more cylindrical. Most vases are symmetrical, so you can check how well you've captured this by holding your drawing against a mirror.

Step 2

To get the perspective right when you draw the neck of the vase, stay in the same position and observe your vase from the same place. Now, start to draw the ellipse of the lip of the vase. Rub out the top of your oval and draw in the curve. Then add the base of the vase.

Step 3

By adding detail to the neck and base, the vase will look more complete. Where is the light hitting your vase? The side away from the light will be darker. Our artist has drawn a line down the left side of the vase and a lighter line down the right side marking where to shade the vase.

Step 4

To create the illusion of depth, as well as shading the side of the vase with hatching lines quite close together, the inside of the lip has also been shaded. Because the light shines on the front of the vase, it highlights there and on the right side of the vase, leaving the left side in shadow.

STILL LIFE
Violin

Tomb paintings from ancient Egypt depict people playing musical instruments, so we know that for thousands of years, music has been a way of life and art, too. Drawing musical instruments, such as the violin, provides artists with the opportunity to capture unique shapes, textures and characteristics.

Step 1

Position the bow of the violin so that you create a triangular composition. Violins have several interesting details to draw, such as the strings, pegs and bridge. However, the shape of the violin's body is the trickiest because it is symmetrical and has cutouts, so start with this shape and then move on to the other details.

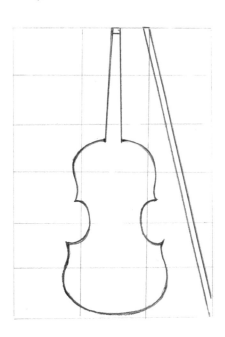

Step 2

Once you're happy with the shape of the violin's body, you can start to add the details – leave the strings until last and focus on the bridge, pegs, tailpiece and the sound holes. You should now have a two-dimensional musical instrument.

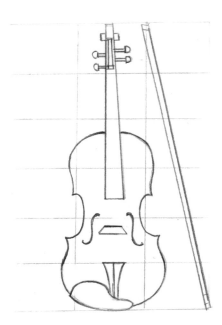

Step 3

To transform your violin into a three-dimensional drawing, you create the depth at the top of the violin. To do this, you can make the line around the top thicker. Add darker lines to the neck of the violin and the strings.

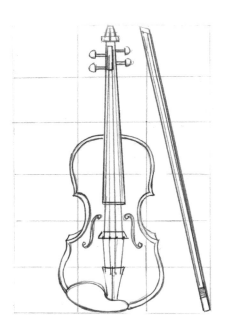

Step 4

While the texture of musical instruments is smooth and you need to add minimal shading to the body, the pegs, tailpiece, fingerboard and chin rest are usually made of a darker wood so will need some shading. The pegs need shading around their bottom edges to convey their depth and quality.

Kitchen Utensils

Creating the illusion of metal can be a difficult skill to master. Light bounces off the surface of the metal, creating reflections. You need to draw the reflections on the utensils exactly as you see them to give them shape and volume.

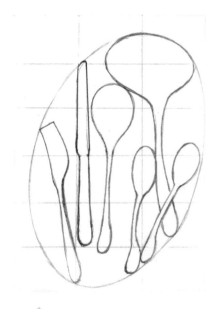

Step 1

Choose an interesting assortment of kitchen utensils. Our artist has chosen a variety of spoons as well as a knife and fork. To get the composition right, she set up the utensils in an oval on her grid.

Step 2

Once you are happy with the composition of your still life, rub out the oval and fill in the details of each utensil. This includes the prongs of the fork, blade of the knife and holes of the slotted spoon.

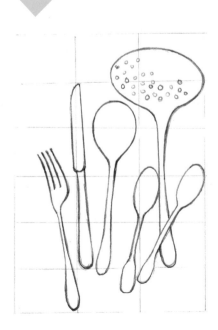

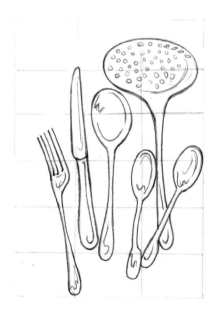

Step 3

The outline of each utensil needs to be made thicker to create depth. Then draw a line within the bowl of each spoon to give them definition. Now look where the light is being reflected the most and what part of each utensil is in shadow. Those parts in shadow need a darker outline. Use a soft pencil to do this.

Step 4

Because metal reflects light, there are lots of highlights that need to be captured in this drawing. You'll need to observe your utensils carefully to see just where these are – shade around them to create the contrast. The utensils also have strong shadows, so you will need to draw these, too.

Fern Plant

The leaves of fern plants are called fronds. If you look closely at the fronds, you will see that each frond is divided into smaller leaflets. These leaflets, which are also called pinnae, are the same shape as the larger frond. This unique characteristic makes ferns interesting to draw.

Step 1

Pick a section of the fern to draw. To find the best composition, you could use your viewfinder. Draw the basic outline of the fern. It makes for a more interesting drawing if you include a frond that has not opened up yet.

Step 2

Start to add the detail to one of the fronds, and the unopened one. You will need to make sure that each pinnae is the same shape as the larger frond. This is intricate work that takes time, and it is important not to rush it.

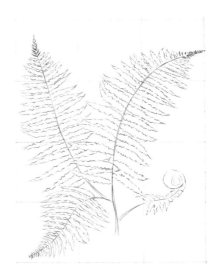

Step 3

Finish all the little pinnae. Notice how our artist has kept the detail of the pinnae even up to the smallest ones at the very top of the stems. Rub out the lines you drew to get the basic leaf shape.

Step 4

Use hatching lines of varying distances to give the leaves their detail. The unfurled frond has some highlights to give it its shape.

Oak Tree

Oak trees are not the world's tallest trees but they can stand an impressive 20 metres high and have a spread of 15 metres wide. While the acorns and leaves are interesting to draw, the bark, with its rough and marked texture, provides a great challenge for those learning to draw.

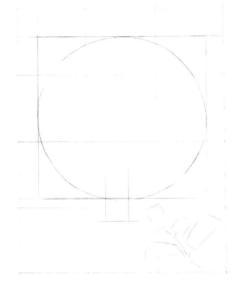

Step 1

Use a ruler and a light pencil to draw a square and a rectangle. Then using this square as your guide, draw a circle within the square. This will be the shape of your tree. Draw the basic outline of your acorn, too.

Step 2

Now draw the detail of your tree and the trunk. You can draw the details of the acorn, too. Leave the circle as it is for now because it will help to keep the shape of the tree. Draw the leaves of the inset of the acorn.

Step 3

The branches of your oak tree need to be drawn in this step as well as the leaves on them. Your tree should begin to look more like an oak tree now. Draw the detail on the acorn inset, such as the veins on the leaves.

Step 4

From a distance you won't be able to see the individual leaves, but rather a mass of leaves, so our artist has added tones to give the tree a dense texture. On the acorn inset, the shading reflects the textured lines found on an acorn.

Water Lily

As a result of their simple, striking beauty, water lilies have been painted and drawn by many artists. Possibly the most famous of these artists is Claude Monet. In 2007, one of Monet's water lily paintings sold for £18.5 million at an auction.

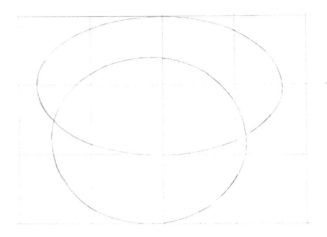

Step 1

This first step is a good exercise in drawing circles and ellipses. If you need to build your drawing confidence, practise drawing these shapes first because they are an integral part of the shape of the water lily. Draw the circle, then draw the ellipse overlapping the top half of the circle.

Step 2

Now draw the petal's of the lily in the circle. The petals are triangular in shape and they vary in size as you move around the circle. Draw the leaf or pad as a triangle cut out from the ellipse.

Step 3

Add more detail to the flower. This includes more of the petals and the centre. Give depth to the lily pad by adding lines just inside the leaf.

Step 4

The combination of shading techniques gives this flower its depth. By using a darker line for the outline of each petal, the flower really stands out. The lily pad is darker than the flower, so this is reflected in the darker shading.

Cactus

These hardy plants have evolved to survive the harsh conditions in which they grow by developing thorns instead of leaves, and ribbed or fluted stems that expand to store water. While cacti may not be the most beautiful plants to draw, they certainly will challenge you.

Step 1

Start with the main stem of the cactus. You can do this with a ruler or freehand, depending on your preference. We've created an inset of the stem so that you can see how to draw this from close-up, too.

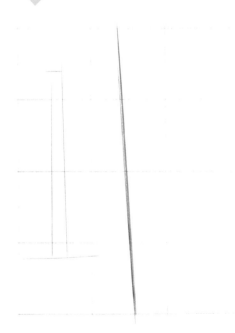

Step 2

Draw the rest of cactus' outline. These are quite straightforward shapes. At this stage of your drawing, the stem is simply a series of lines.

Step 3

When you look at the close-up of the stem, you can see there are lines to show the folds. From far away, these look like plain lines, which you need to now draw. You can draw the thorns on the inset at this stage, too.

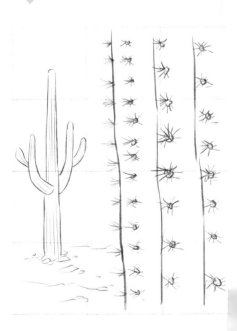

Step 4

Shade the main plant to give it its definition. Because these plants are found in sunny places, the Sun will naturally create a lot of highlights and shadows that you need to capture on the main plant and on the inset image, too.

Houses

One of the first things that most people learn to draw is a house: a square with a triangular roof, little square windows and a rectangular door. A modern house is built using many different materials and to capture these, along with the house's key features, can be a fascinating exercise.

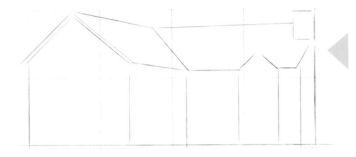

Step 1

Use your ruler to draw a rectangle frame. This will help you to gauge the proportions of your house. You can then use a ruler to draw the outline of the house. This is a good exercise in perspective and in getting the angles of the house correct.

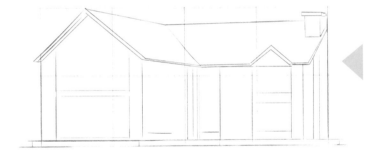

Step 2

Again using your ruler, draw further details such as the gutters, windows and chimney of the house.

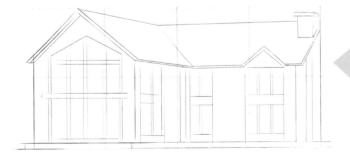

Step 3

The detail of the large window at the front of the house should now be drawn: again you can do this using your ruler. The other window panes can also now be drawn.

Step 4

To create the glass of the windows, you need to add tone to the drawing. Note how the light hits the window to create highlights. The roof of the house has been given texture by cross-hatching. Once you have shaded the house, you need to add the shadow it creates in front of the building.

Haunted House

If you are happy with your drawing of a house on pages 72–73, you could try to draw this haunted house, too. Concentrate on drawing the bricks and mortar of the house. Use tone to create a haunted look and feel.

Step 1

Draw the basic outline of your house using a ruler. To get the angles of the pitched roof correct, you can use the perpendicular line of the side of the house as your guide.

Step 2

In this step, you should complete the basic structure of the house and fill in details to give it shape. The spire can easily be drawn in from the triangle. Draw the outline of the porch, too.

Step 3

In this step, your house will really begin to take shape. Add the roof windows and the window in the spire. Then add the remaining window at the front and sides of the house.

Step 4

There are many different textures to try to capture in this picture. There are bricks, wood and glass. Our artist has used different lines to create these textures, for example dark lines to create the bricks, finer vertical lines to capture the wood, and a combination of dark and light hatching for the glass and dark shadowed areas for the foliage texture. To transform the building into a haunted house, windows are broken, bricks are missing and the porch is rickety.

ARCHITECTURE
Street

A busy street with a mixture of different buildings can make a striking drawing. Focus on all the different elements of the scene, from people and pets to objects such as cars, bicycles, motorcycles, trees and signs. You'll need to understand how to use perspective to draw this image.

Step 1

The buildings in this street appear to get smaller as you look further down the street, giving the impression of distance. This illusion is created by perspective. To begin, draw the lines of the shop fronts. The lines should lead towards the vanishing point to the back of the image and those on the vertical and horizontal lines, too.

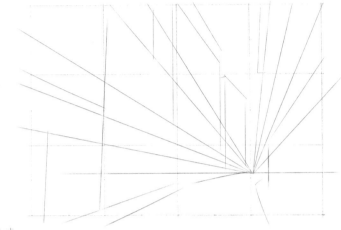

Step 2

Now you can begin to draw the shop fronts and details. This street has several buildings with balconies, awnings and different signage. You don't need to add the people until the next step. Focus now on correctly drawing the buildings.

Step 3

Start to add further detail to the buildings. Lines added to features such as awnings give them their shape. The basic outline of the people can also be added at this stage.

Step 4

To create the perspective, your buildings should pale as you move down the street. You can see how the buildings towards the back of the street are quite light in comparison to those near the front. Shading also gives the different building materials their characteristics and the people their shape. It's not necessary to draw the minute details of the people, but you need to correctly proportion their bodies.

Castle

Castle Neuschwanstein is a nineteenth-century Romanesque Revival
palace that is found in Bavaria, Germany. The castle is said to have
inspired the castle logo seen at the start of most Disney films.
Its turrets and spires are classic architectural features to draw.

Step 1

Use your ruler to draw the basic
geometric shapes of the castle.
These are several rectangles,
triangles and cubes. Draw in the
basic outline of the trees, too.

Step 3

Fill in the details such as the
windows in this next step. Your
drawing should begin to look like
the famous castle now. Make sure
all the details are added so that
only the shading stage is left.

Step 2

In this step, you can transform
your basic shapes into the Gothic
features of the castle. Keep checking
your reference to make sure you are
drawing the angles correctly. Add
further detail to the trees on the
left-hand side and in the front, too.

Step 4

Our artist has used shading to great advantage here. He has added darker values to the pitched roofs. To give the roofs a smooth texture, he has shaded them and rubbed over them carefully with his finger. To create the texture of the trees, the artist has used very dark shading.

Feet

Many people struggle to draw feet, and others will avoid drawing them altogether! Just as you would draw any object by breaking it down into simple shapes, drawing feet can be approached in the same way.

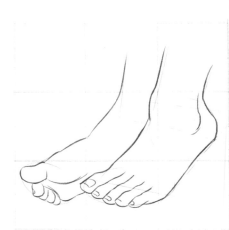

Step 1

When drawing feet or any part of the body, you need to be aware of the anatomical proportions. The sole of your foot is roughly the same length as your forearm, and if your foot is bent upwards, your hand should fit on top of your foot. Once you've worked out the proportions, you can draw the basic shapes of the ankles, ball of the foot and heels.

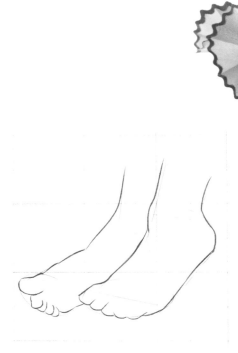

Step 2

Using the basic shapes from step 1 you can start to draw the details. Start with the basic outline of the foot. Notice how the foot goes in at the ankle and is slightly rounded at the front. You can draw the tips of the toes, too. Our subject's second toe is slightly curled inwards: this makes drawing it trickier but ultimately, it makes your drawing more interesting.

Step 3

In this step, the feet really do begin to look like feet because the toes are now defined. Be sure to get the proportions of the toes correct – not everyone's toes go from big to small! The details of the toenails are also added in this step. The folds of skin under the right foot are drawn here, giving the foot its curved shape.

Step 4

To complete the drawing, our
artist has given the outline a much
darker line. The feet are shaded
using a combination of hatching
and cross-hatching, with the
sets of lines at varying distances,
depending on the light. Our artist
has created highlights by leaving
some areas white and also by using
soft, widely set, cross-hatching.

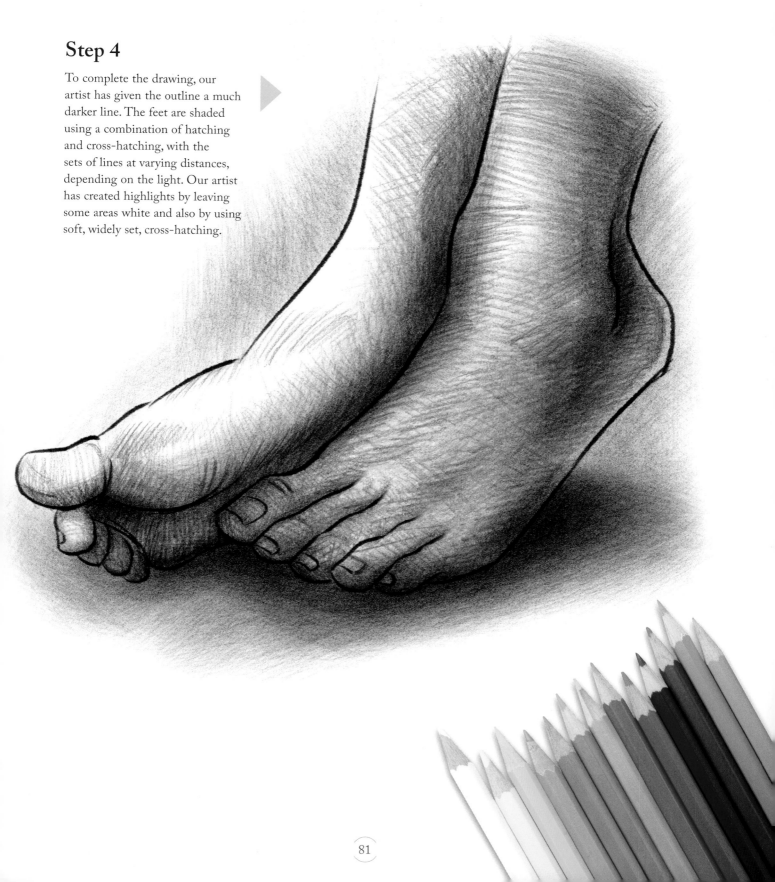

Hands

The hands you create in a drawing tell the viewer a great deal about the person to whom they belong. Rough hands, for example, may show that a person does a lot of manual labour, while wrinkled, dry hands usually belong to an older person.

Step 1

If you're drawing the back of the hands, you can break them down by using a trapezoid for the wrist and top of the hands, and rectangles of different sizes of the fingers. Our artist has drawn the thumb and little finger as separate rectangles, and used just one larger rectangle for the remaining three fingers.

Step 2

When adding your outline, remember that the hand is broader at the fingers than at the wrist, but it is deeper at the wrist. Notice, too, how our artist has captured the ball of the thumb, which makes it a mobile unit. Remember to pay careful attention to the relative sizes of the fingers.

Step 3

Add the fingernails, which are slightly oval in shape. The fingers have two joints, which are captured by lines. Our model's hands are quite wrinkled, showing her age. Notice how, at this stage, lines are drawn to show the wrinkles on the hands, but they will also later be shaded.

Step 4

Along with wrinkles, as people age, the veins in their hands become more prominent. These have been depicted by adding darker values around the veins and highlights. The texture of skin is captured by hatching lines that are not too close together.

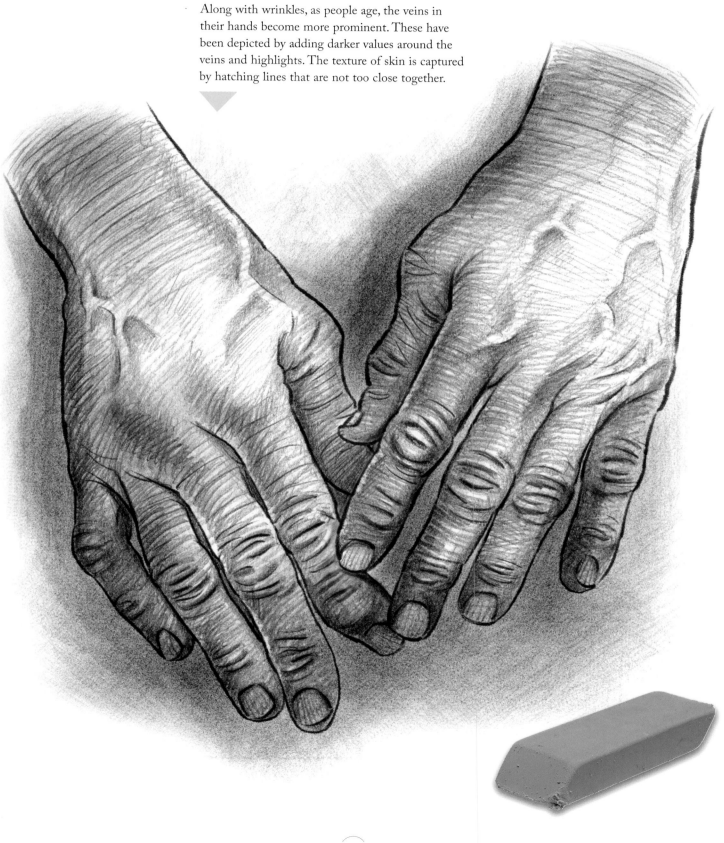

Person Kicking a Ball

Capturing movement means not only achieving an anatomically correct body, but also conveying the way the person moves. This footballer is a good example to practise because not only is he kicking the ball, but his arms are also positioned to keep his balance.

Step 1

Draw a cross onto which to draw your footballer. The vertical line should go down the centre of the torso while the horizontal will show you where to draw the waist. The footballer's body can be drawn using basic shapes: a circle for the head, a square for the torso, a trapezoid for each arm and rectangles for the legs.

Step 2

Now soften your basic shapes to create the outline of your footballer. The head becomes an oval while the arms and torso are given definition.

Step 3

Add the folds of the footballer's clothes – these help to give the drawing the illusion of movement. The player's facial features, such as hair, the nose and eyes have also been added. It's important to get the proportions of these right, so you can always practise these during the portraiture exercises. The shadow under the ball helps to transform it from a circle into a ball.

Step 4

To complete your drawing and create the illusion of movement, pay careful attention to where you draw the shadows. They will be behind the player's right arm and bent legs. Notice too how the left side of his body is highlighted.

Ballet Dancer

Ballet dancers train for many hours each day. Their bodies are toned to perfection and are strong but lithe. The arabesque is a classic ballet position that shows off the dancer's strength as well as the grace and beauty of the ballet.

Step 1

Draw a cross to help you to gauge the proportions of the dancer. One line needs to go through her waist while the other divides her torso in half. Draw the basic shapes that you see.

Step 2

Add the shape of the dancer's head and leotard. By drawing the leotard you are giving her legs definition, too.

Step 3

Draw the facial features, and details of the hands and shoes.

Step 4

To complete your drawing, you will need to add more detail to the leotard and shoes. The dancer's bust is given shape by using a darker line. The shadow drawn behind the ballerina gives her movement. The hatching used on her legs, along with the highlights, give her muscles definition.

PORTRAITURE

Eyes

It is very rare that a person's eyes are identical. Sometimes, the difference between a person's eyes is great, with some people even having different coloured eyes. At other times, the eyes are almost, but not quite, identical. Drawing eyes means first seeing the difference and then capturing it so that the eyes really do become the 'window' of your subject's soul.

Step 1

To begin your drawing, draw your grid so that you can work out where to position the eyes. Think about the proportions of the eye. Each half of a face is two eye-widths wide, with the eye taking up one eye width, and then half an eye width on the outside of the eye. There is another half an eye width between the eye and the mid-point of the head. Now draw the basic shapes that you can see. Our subject's eyes are oval in shape and the eyebrows are quite round, too.

Step 2

Now draw the eye sockets, eyelids and the pupils. Remember that the pupils expand and contract, depending on how light the subject's surroundings are.

Step 3

To give the shape of the eye further definition, use a softer pencil to go around the outline of the eye. The eyelid is always in shadow, so this line needs to be darker. Sometimes, you may be so far away that you cannot see your subject's eyelashes. If you can see them, draw them now. You can also start to draw some of the texture of the eyebrows. Look carefully at the irises of the eyes. They have a darker ring around the outside, which you need to draw.

Step 4

To complete your artwork, you will need to see where the light is reflected in the bottom half of the iris. Take your kneadable eraser and mould it into a fine point to make these highlights. Note how the light is reflected in the pupils. You can capture these reflections by darkening the rest of the pupil. Add some shading to the lower eyelid and to define the socket. Shade around the eyes, especially the inner eye, which will be in shadow – this will help to shape the bridge of the nose. Darken the eyelashes and eyebrows to give them definition. In this drawing, you can see how the eyes are not exactly the same: the eye on the right is slightly rounder and larger than the one on the left.

Young Man

Capturing a likeness is one of the most difficult parts of drawing a portrait. A likeness is achieved if the proportion is accurate. The subject's eyes must be just the right distance apart and the mouth not too big or too small.

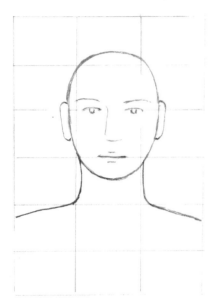

Step 1

Start by drawing the basic shape of the head. Heads are usually oval in shape so capture the roundness at the top and let it taper down to the bottom. Draw in the outline of the neck and shoulders.

Step 2

This is a difficult stage – now you need to perfect the proportions. The base of the nose should sit in the bottom half of the oval shape. If you divide this again in half, that's where the mouth will be. The eyes are on the horizontal line that divided your oval in half. The base of the ear should be drawn in line with the bottom of the nose and the top of the ear should be in line with the eyebrows. Your subject's ears should be flat against the side of the head.

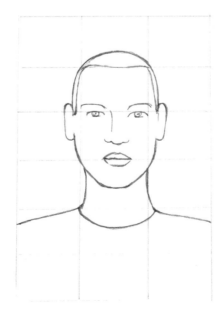

Step 3

Start to add details such as the hair and clothes. The subject's hair is short so our artist has drawn this by using repeated circles and squiggles. Start to shade the features, such as the lips and eyes. The definition of the cheekbones can be achieved by drawing lines to mark them. Shading on the jaw line gives it some definition and shape.

Step 4

Now you can begin to bring your portrait to life. Look carefully at where the light shines and shadows form on the face. The top of the nose and middle of the forehead are lighter, as are the cheeks. However, under the nose and lips it is darker. The irises of the eyes are very dark, almost as dark as the pupils. Note how the shadows in the eye sockets give shape to the bridge of the nose.

Old Man

The ageing process differs from person to person, depending on race, diet and the environment in which the person lives. As people grow older, they start to develop lines around their eyes, with bags under their eyes and skin imperfections becoming more visible. Using the portrait from pages 90-91, you can see how the man in that portrait will age to become the man in this portrait.

Step 1

Start with the basic shape of the head and shoulders. The subject's face is rounder than it was on page 90.

Step 2

In the same way that you drew the features in your portrait on page 90, do the same now. Pay careful attention to the nose, which will have grown as the man has aged. Also, the eye sockets have become more prominent with age and the subject's hairline has receded.

Step 3

During the ageing process, the cheeks begin to sag, giving the appearance of jowls. These are outlined in this step. The outline of the subject's eyes is also drawn here – the tissue around the eyes has started to sag, creating 'bags' under the eyes.

Step 4

The ageing process is made clear by adding values to the drawing. The contrast between light and dark is greater, giving the appearance of aged skin, especially around the mouth and jowl area. Because the eyelids have started to droop, the eyelashes are less visible than previously. The hair is also lighter than before because it has started to grey.

Self-Portrait

A self-portrait is a representation of the artist, created by the artist. One of the earliest self-portraits from 1433 is Portrait of a Man in a Turban by Jan van Eyck. Self-portraiture is difficult because you must scrutinise your own features, and then make your personal, private observations a very public act.

Step 1

One of the most important stages in drawing a self-portrait is to observe your features. This is perhaps most easily done by working with a photograph and a grid. Once you have scrutinised these, you can start as you would any portrait. Draw your head, neck and shoulders.

Step 2

Start to draw the features of your face. Your eyes should be halfway down your face. Draw the outlines of your hair. Note how the hair is obscuring the subject's ear, and her hairline is quite high.

Step 3

Begin to add further detail such as dark lines for your hair. Drawing the pupils of your eyes and lightly shading the inner eye will give your nose shape. Darken the outline of the lips to give them definition.

Step 4

Shade your features to add depth to your self-portrait. While dark lines are drawn to create the texture of hair, there are also highlights to show how the light is reflected off it. To create texture around the parting, our artist has darkened this area. Try to capture your age realistically. This artist has youthful skin and so minimal shading was added to her skin.

ANIMALS
Cat

Much of the time, cats are drawn sleeping or resting. They are drawn in this way because cats do not keep still for very long, so drawing them can be difficult! To make your drawing experience easier, capture your cat in a photograph so that their restless behaviour doesn't impede your art.

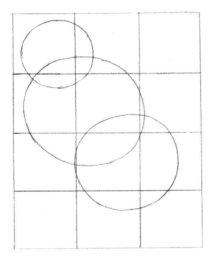

Step 1

The cat we chose to draw is sitting upright. To draw her, you will need to create three circles. Notice the different sizes of the circles, the top circle, which is for the head, is much smaller than the one that will be used for the trunk.

Step 2

In this step, you will need to give your circles a feline shape. Start with the head, by drawing the ears. They are pointed so a basic triangular shape will help to capture them. Draw your horizontal and vertical line so that drawing the face will be easier. Then add the legs and paws. The legs need to be thicker at the top and taper down into the paws. Draw the tail in this step, too.

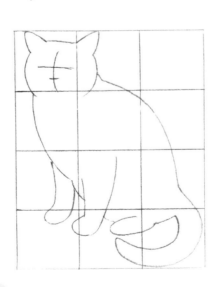

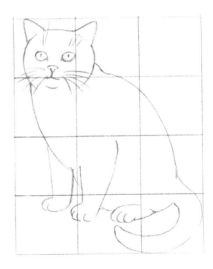

Step 3

Now you can add the facial features of your cat. Cats generally have large eyes but smaller pupils. Add the cat's mouth and whiskers at this stage.

Step 4

Draw the cat's whisker spots to give its face a more feline appearance. Now you can start to give the fur its texture. This is a time-consuming job because the shading needs to reflect the cat's short, but plentiful, fur. Give the ears their depth, too, by shading the inside of the ears while also creating contrasting highlights around the top.

ANIMALS

Dog

Dogs are said to be mans' best friend. Like cats, dogs do not sit still for long periods and so drawing them may be difficult. Try to capture your dog in a photograph so that you can spend time drawing it accurately.

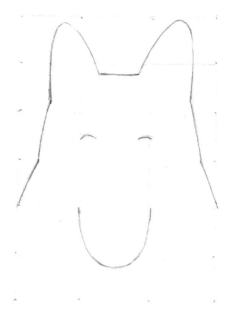

Step 1

Once you've drawn your grid on your photograph and on your paper, start to draw the basic shapes you see in the dog. The ears are triangular while the mouth area is an upright ellipse. Draw marks for the eyes.

Step 2

Add more detail to the dog, such as its eyes, nose and the basic shape of its tongue. By drawing a line at the top of the head, the ears will be given a more definite shape.

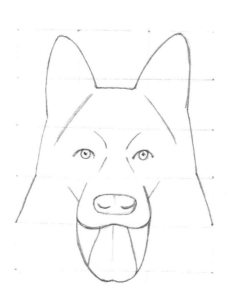

Step 3

Now you can draw more detail in the eyes. Just like human eyes, a dog's eyes have a darker pupil and a lighter iris, but more importantly, the eye socket needs to be given depth. You can also start to draw some of the details of the ear and some of the fur in this step.

Step 4

The long-haired alsatian dog really comes to life in this step through the addition of eyes and fur. The long fur is created using long lines that are close together in some places but further apart in others. The further apart lines give the fur depth and fullness. Look carefully at the way in which our artist has shaded the eyes, nose and mouth area. The tongue is light but the inside of the mouth is much darker.

Stag

There are 44 different species of deer. With the exception of the Chinese Water Deer, all males have antlers. The older the stag, the larger its antlers will be. When drawing a stag, you will need to depict the size and shape of the antlers accurately and in proportion to the rest of the stag's body.

Step 1

Start with the basic shape of the head, legs and trunk of your stag. The stag has a long neck, which gives it its characteristic bovine look.

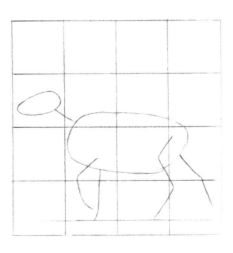

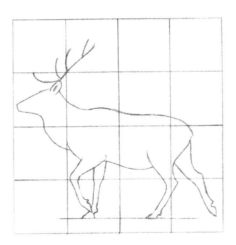

Step 2

Transform your basic shapes into a stag by drawing the shape of the neck, ears and legs. You can draw the stag's antlers in this step, too.

Step 3

This step focuses on correctly drawing the stag's antlers. Antlers tell us much about a stag, including its age, so they need to be accurately drawn. This stag has long antlers, so its body should be that of an older stag.

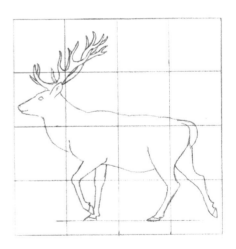

Step 4

Shade the stag's horns to capture how they twist and turn. The darker insides give the antlers their unique shape. The deer has short fur so the texture of this can be captured by using shorter shading lines and leaving some areas of paper white.

Eagle

There are approximately 10,000 species of bird in the world. The variety of shapes, colours, sizes, movements and contexts means that anyone with an interest in drawing, will find birds challenging and inspiring subjects. And none more so than the majestic eagle.

Step 1

Nothing is more majestic than an eagle in full flight. You can really see the power of the bird's wings when they are fully open. Start with the basic body shape and then draw the wings and tail shape of the bird.

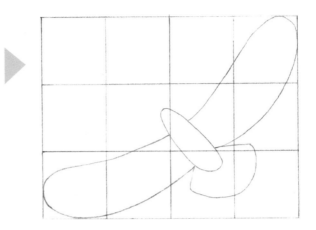

Step 2

Add the head and beak to your bird, as well as the pointed wing feathers. When you are happy with the shape of the wings, you can rub out the initial lines.

Step 3

In this step, you can add the tail feathers. The individual feathers should cover the fan shape that you drew in step 1. You can also now draw the eagle's powerful legs and talons.

Step 4

Now you need to capture the texture of each feather. The eagle's wing feathers are longer than the tail feathers and the feathers on the bird's neck and body. The wings closer to the bird's body will be in shadow, so they should be shaded with a darker tone.

Butterfly

There are four stages in a butterfly's life cycle: egg, larva, pupa and adult. With their brightly coloured wings and fluttering flight, adult butterflies are some of the most attractive insects. You could use this drawing of a Monarch butterfly as a starting point for a series of drawings depicting these beautiful creatures.

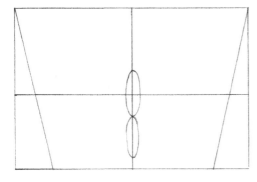

Step 1

Drawing a butterfly is an exercise in symmetry. To create the symmetry of the insect, first draw a square. Then draw triangles on the sides of your square to change it into a polygon. Bisect the polygon in half vertically and horizontally. Draw the thorax of the butterfly so that it fits on the bisecting lines where they cross in the centre.

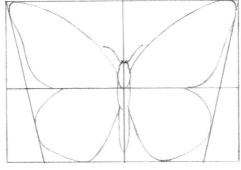

Step 2

Using your polygon as a guide to help you with the symmetry, draw the butterfly's wings. Try to keep them identical on each side. Draw the butterfly's antennae, too.

Step 3

You can start to draw the markings on the thorax and the markings on the wings. Monarch butterflies have very distinct markings, which you must try to capture at this stage.

Step 4

Once you have drawn in all the markings on your butterfly, you can start to shade it. The body will be dark with highlights to capture the segmented tail. The markings are captured by intricate shading around the highlights, which are created by the white of the paper showing through.

Motorbike

These machines are made up of many different materials, from leather seats to metal bodywork and rubber tyres. They are also very different in style and shape, depending on the type of motorbike. Capturing the smooth lines of a superbike is a great way to practise drawing angles.

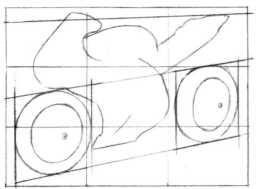

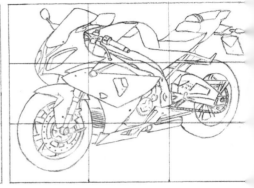

Step 1

Drawing the bike at the angle shown above means that your viewer can see all of the machine. Divide your drawing space as indicated above. Note how the angles of the middle and bottom lines give your bike perspective. They also help to keep the bike in proportion. Draw the wheels – they will be slightly elliptical in shape because of the viewpoint. Draw the rest of the bike's basic shape to fit within your lines.

Step 2

Now add the details of the bodywork so that your bike starts to take the form of a powerful superbike.

Step 3

Add the details of the wheels and front of the bike, and also draw the machine's seat and licence plate.

Step 4

From the greasy chain and leather seat to the metallic bodywork, to capture the different materials used, you need to shade to give each material its texture. Our artist has left the glass of the windshield as a highlight and shaded elsewhere. Note how the highlights on the exhaust create its rounded metallic look.

Formula One Car

With drivers experiencing forces of 3G and sometimes more, Formula One cars are the ultimate speed machines. Speeds in excess of 350 kilometres per hour are achieved by great feats of mechanical engineering and chassis design. Pay tribute to the sophisticated design of these cars by drawing one.

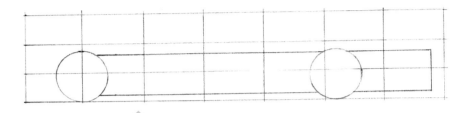

Step 1

This exercise is truly a lesson in drawing geometric shapes. The basic car can be broken down into a long rectangle and two circles. Note how the circle on the left is drawn right at the end of the rectangle.

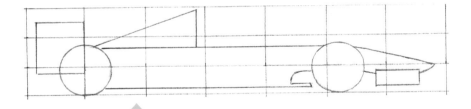

Step 2

In this step, a square is added for the rear wing, while a triangle gives the nose cone its shape. A triangle is also drawn to give the chassis its aerodynamic shape.

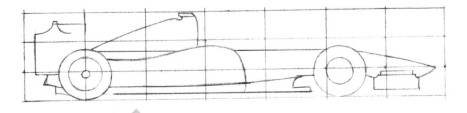

Step 3

Now transform the basic shapes into the car by adding detail. Start with the tyres, then move from the rear of the car through to the nose cone.

Step 4

Once you are happy with your drawing, you will need to give the bodywork its glossy carbon look and the rubber of the tyres their muted rubber look.

Step 5

Shading also gives the car its depth. Our artist has used numerous highlights to make sure all the curves of the bodywork have been captured.

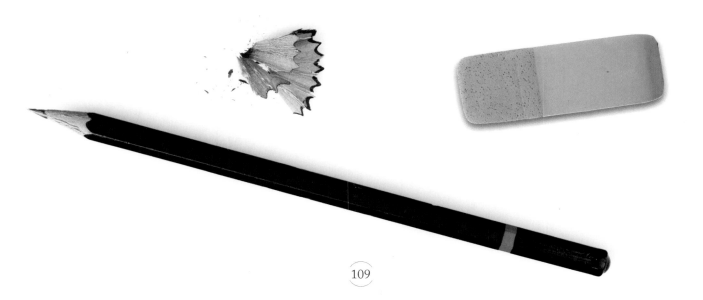

Steam Train

Steam trains became popular in the early nineteenth century and although they have today largely been replaced by electric engines, they are still admired for their mechanical ingenuity. With a funnel billowing steam and their wheel sets moving swiftly, steam trains provide artists with a picture of mechanical engineering that has stood the test of time.

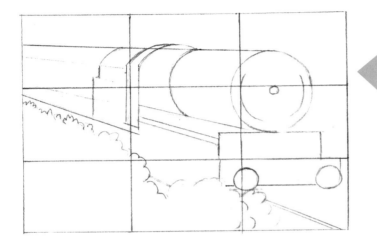

Step 1

The engine is definitely the most interesting part of the train. Our artist has drawn the train as if it were travelling around a bend, into the page. Can you see the basic shapes of the engine? Start by drawing these and the outline of shrubs on the track – these obscure some of the engine, so by creating them now, you will understand which details of the engine can't be shown.

Step 2

Now transform the basic cylinders into the train by adding details. By drawing the funnel, your engine immediately looks more like a train. Add the wheels to the track in this step, too.

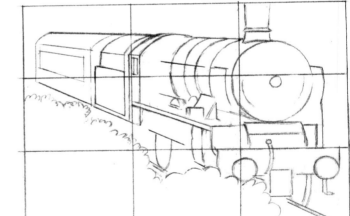

Step 3

Now add further details, such as windows, to the carriages and greater detail to the engine. Your drawing should really start to look like a steam train now.

Step 4

Due to the size of the train, to capture all its detail can be time consuming. However, it is incredibly rewarding. With the basic details of your engine complete, start to shade it. As with other machines, there are many materials used to make a steam train and their unique textures need to be captured.

Helicopter

People have always been fascinated by flying. Greek legend tells of a man, Icarus, who flew too close to the Sun, melting his waxen wings. Today's flying machines include space shuttles, aeroplanes and helicopters. A helicopter's lift and thrust is supplied by the rotors, allowing the aircraft to fly upwards, downwards, forwards and backwards.

Step 1

By drawing the helicopter at this angle, you can see more of it. The basic shape of the cockpit can be difficult to get right, but once you have correctly drawn the angle, the entire helicopter should have its identifying shape. Add the helicopter's rotors at this stage, too.

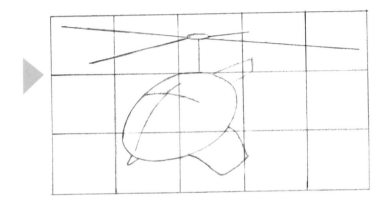

Step 2

Add the tail of the helicopter and the windows. By adding lines to the roof of the cockpit and detail to the landing skids, your basic shape will start to look more like a helicopter.

Step 3

Spend time working on the main rotor now. The blades need to be given a three-dimensional look and the rotor mast should be added in this step, too.

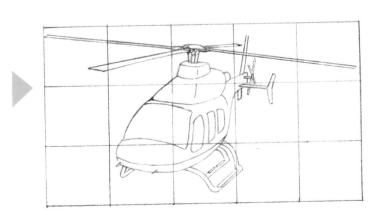

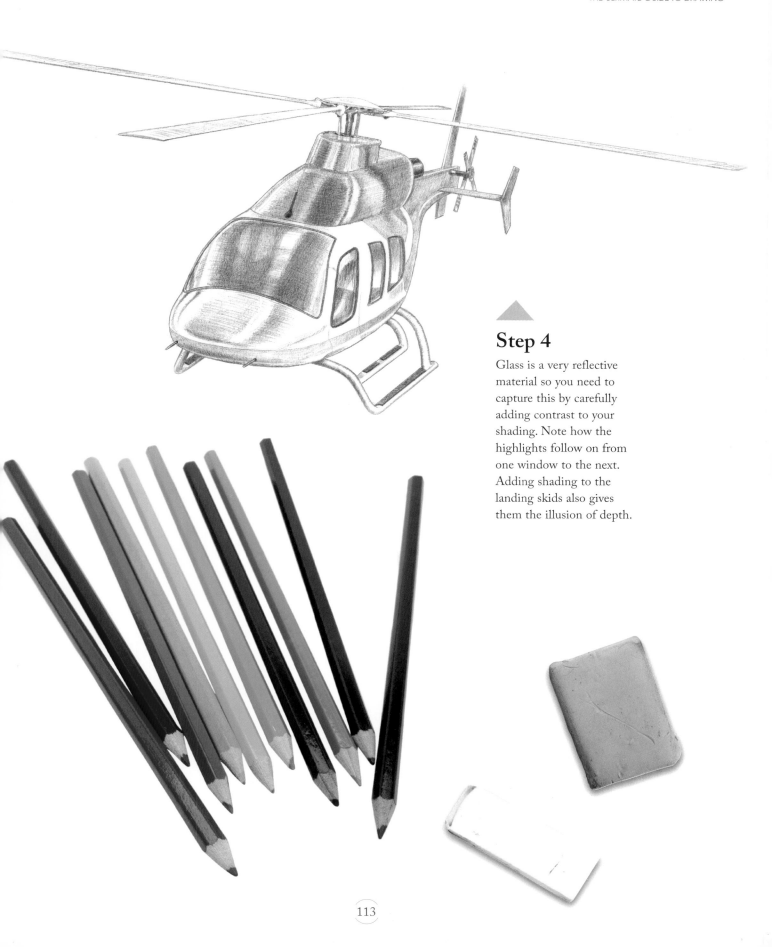

Step 4

Glass is a very reflective material so you need to capture this by carefully adding contrast to your shading. Note how the highlights follow on from one window to the next. Adding shading to the landing skids also gives them the illusion of depth.

Dragon

When drawing beasts of fantasy, there really are no rules about how they should look. Drawing a dragon is a great exercise in imaginative drawing. These beasts can take many shapes and sizes, some have wings and spined backs, while others do not.

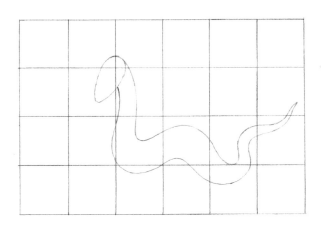

Step 1

Consider how you want your dragon to look, then draw its basic head and body shape. Our dragon's body looks rather like a fattened snake.

Step 2

Draw the dragon's wings. Notice how our artist has drawn the dragon's right wing to account for the viewpoint. Use a cross to mark out where the facial features will go.

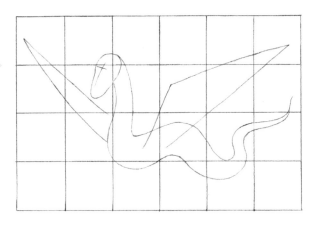

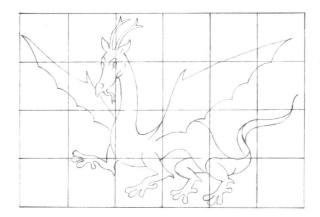

Step 3

Now draw the legs, horns, tongue, ears and facial features. Unlike in human portraiture, the nose is nearer to the bottom of the face and the mouth is almost invisible. Add detail to the wings and body to give them shape.

Step 4

Add the finishing touches to your dragon.
Draw spikes on its spine and claws on its
feet before you bring your dragon to life
by adding values. The contrast between
light and dark values give the dragon's
neck and wings their texture.

Unicorn

Unicorns are one of the most beautiful creatures of fantasy fiction. To draw a unicorn, artists must capture the unicorn's grace and ethereal beauty. One of the best ways to start is to study the anatomy of a horse before adding the magical elements that transform the animal into a unicorn.

Step 1

Draw the basic shapes of the unicorn's body. Like a horse, a unicorn can be created by using a combination of different-sized ovals for the head, neck and trunk.

Step 2

Add the unicorn's four legs and tail. Now add the eye, ear and horn. The horn is probably the unicorn's more distinguishing feature. Without it, the unicorn will look just like a horse.

Step 3

Now add the unicorn's mane and other hair. By adding hair to the tail and face, the unicorn is given a distinctive look. Add the rest of the facial features and detail to the horn.

Step 4

Much like a well-groomed horse, the unicorn's body is muscular but graceful. While the creature's grace is captured through the pose used, the muscles and texture of its fur are captured through shading, in particular with highlights. Shading also gives the unicorn's ears depth and its hooves a glossy look.

Mermaid

Mermaids feature in many fantasy books and films. They are creatures with the upper body of a female human and the tail of a fish. They are interesting to draw because you draw the human form but also capture the texture and shape of the mermaid's fish tail.

Step 1

Use a grid to ensure you get the proportions of the mermaid right – this is especially important in this drawing. Draw the basic shapes of the human upper body and the tail. Our mermaid is sitting on a rock.

Step 2

Now add the arms and nose of the mermaid. Carefully draw her delicate hands. Separate the tail fin from the tail in this step, too.

Step 3

Add the mermaid's hair so that her upper body begins to take a female form. Add more detail to the hands, too.

Step 4

There are many textures to capture in this final step. These include the rock, water, scales and the mermaid's hair and skin. You'll need to shade this very carefully to capture these textures. Notice where the highlights and shadows fall. The right side of the body is in shadow, so the hair on that side appears darker than on the left.

Fossil

Drawing fossils is often left to palaeontological illustrators, who specialise in drawing these ancient remains. Their primary goal is to recreate the fossil so it is scientifically correct. However, turning something, such as an ammonite, from a scientific artwork into an aesthetically-pleasing drawing can be creatively stimulating.

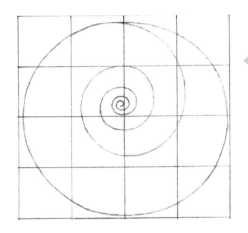

Step 1

The ammonite has a spiral shell that ends abruptly, without tapering off. To begin the drawing, draw a circle as the starting point. Next, draw the spiral starting at the top of the circle, spiralling into the centre.

Step 2

Draw the line where the shell ends, then rub out the part of the shell that you don't want in your drawing. This will leave you with the basic shape of your ammonite.

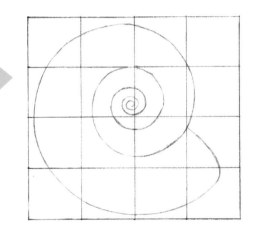

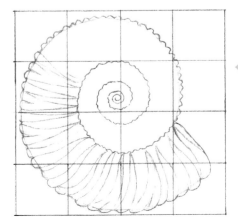

Step 3

The ammonite shell is not smooth, so to add texture, jagged outer lines are drawn over the initial outlines. Using large, uneven whorls, the shell is given its texture.

Step 4

Once the entire shell is complete, you can add shading. Our artist has used contrast to create the pattern of the shell. The inside of the whorls are shaded more deeply where the fossil is in shadow, but lighter where there are highlights. This shading also creates the impression that the middle of the ammonite is very slightly depressed.

Neanderthal Man

Neanderthal man is the closest prehistoric relative to human beings. Through excavations and the unearthing of Neanderthal remains, palaeontologists have been able to reconstruct Neanderthal man. You can draw Neanderthal man by looking closely at its facial features and applying portraiture skills.

Step 1

While the head of most people is usually oval in shape, that of Neanderthal man is somewhat rounder and longer than a human's. His neck is also thicker and shorter so it looks almost as though the head is balancing on the shoulders. You may find it easier to use a grid to draw this portrait. Using a photograph as a reference, draw the basic outline of the head and shoulders of the prehistoric man.

Step 2

Start to draw the facial features, paying attention to your photograph to get the proportions correct. Neanderthal's chin and forehead sloped backwards compared to that of a modern man's and the nose is larger, too. These differences are subtle but they will give your portrait its Neanderthal appearance. Because the Neanderthal's nose is larger than a modern-day human's, the lips appear larger, too.

Step 3

Add the basic outline of the hair, both on the top of the head and on the face. Lines on the forehead will give the skin its texture and the eyes their sunken look. Now thicken your subject's eyebrows and add 'bags' under the eyes.

Step 4

The hair of the Neanderthal man is coarse and unruly compared with modern man. This can be reflected by adding tone. Here, our artist has used hatching lines but she has varied the spaces between them to give the hair its coarse appearance. The facial hair is curlier and so smaller circles and squiggles are used to create this texture. The shading on the forehead and around the eyes gives the skin its puffy, weathered look. The left side of the face is in shadow, so darker than the right, which has more highlights.

Fruit and Vegetables

Drawing with coloured pencils will really bring out the unique qualities of each fruit and vegetable. To draw in colour you need to get the outline of your drawing correct in pencil first, before adding the colour as you would tone.

Step 1

Begin by drawing your bowl, which is an ellipse. Then draw the basic shapes of the fruit and vegetables, which include circles and ovals.

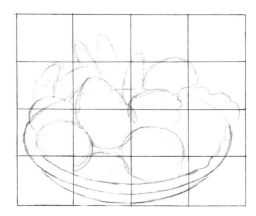

Step 3

The shapes of the smaller fruits, such as grapes, and the details of the larger fruit and vegetables have been drawn. We can see the pineapple, carrots, bananas and turnip quite clearly. The shapes breaking out of the bowl also make the drawing more interesting.

Step 2

Now draw the outline of the fruit and vegetables in more detail. Our artist has carefully positioned the fruit and vegetables so that the most interesting part of each is in the foreground, and so that there is a great variety of colour.

Step 4

Look carefully to see where the
light is falling on your bowl. As
well as capturing the colour of
each fruit and vegetable, you will
need to pay attention to what part
of the fruit is in the light and
what part is in shadow.

Landscapes

From little children to professional artists, most people have tried to draw a landscape at one time or another. To draw a successful landscape, composition is crucial. You need to decide where to place your focal point, aiming to position it within the golden ratio.

Step 1

Decide on your composition. It may be helpful to do a couple of thumbnail sketches to get it right. Once you've decided that your composition works, draw the outline. The fence in this artwork draws the reader into the painting and the perspective gives the illusion of distance.

Step 2

Now sketch the details of the fence and some of the other features of the landscape. You will also need to draw any rugged areas of land at this point.

Step 3

Continue drawing the landscape, adding more detail, such as the trees and grassy outcrops. The hills will start to take shape, too.

Step 4

With the details drawn in, it's time to add colour.
Obviously the colour will give a different warmth
and feel to your landscape, depending on the colours
you use. Use lighter colours towards the back of
the drawing to give the landscape perspective.

Index